I WILL FOLLOW
You,
O GOD

Embracing Him As Lord
in Your Private Worship

JERRY BRIDGES

WATERBROOK
PRESS

I WILL FOLLOW YOU, O GOD
PUBLISHED BY WATERBROOK PRESS
2375 Telstar Drive, Suite 160
Colorado Springs, Colorado 80920
A division of Random House, Inc.

ISBN 1-57856-518-9

Library of Congress Cataloging-in-Publication Data
Bridges, Jerry.
   I will follow you, O God : embracing him as Lord in your private worship / by Jerry Bridges.—
1st ed.
      p. cm.
   Includes bibliographical references and index.
   ISBN 1-57856-518-9
      1. God—Worship and love—Meditations. 2. Christian life—Meditations. 3. Fear of God—
Meditations. I. Title.

BV4817 .B675 2001
248.3—dc21

                                                                        2001026829

Printed in the United States of America
2001—First Edition

10 9 8 7 6 5 4 3 2 1

CONTENTS

Part III: *I Will Follow You, O God...*
       Living All of Life Under Your Authority

Part IV: *I Will Follow You, O God...*
       Delighting in Genuine Obedience

If the LORD is God, follow him.

1 KINGS 18:21

I will give them an undivided heart and put a new spirit in them;
I will remove from them their heart of stone and give them a heart of flesh.
Then they will follow my decrees and be careful to keep my laws.
They will be my people, and I will be their God.

EZEKIEL 11:19-20

Following God Begins
with Fearing God

Two decades ago, while doing research for a book on god-liness, I came across John Murray's statement that "the fear of God is the soul of godliness." My attention was arrested, and I began a small study on the fear of God. That continuing study resulted in 1997 in the book *The Joy of Fearing God.*

In that book I explain that a profound sense of awe toward God is undoubtedly the dominant element in the attitude or set of emotions that the Bible calls "the fear of God." I note a popular definition of fearing God—"reverential awe"—and conclude that this is indeed a good definition. I quote John Murray's further observation that the fear of God "consists in awe, reverence, honor, and worship." I state that this fear of God is an attitude as well as a mix of various emotions, and that whether we think of it more as a complex set of emotions or as an attitude, the important thing is that this mix is to be *determinative.* The emotions and attitude should determine the way we relate to God— the way we obey Him, trust Him, and worship Him…the way we *follow Him*. Properly fearing God is more than just a feeling or attitude; it's a feeling or attitude that changes our lives.

AN UNMISTAKABLE LINK

When I began studying the fear of God, the first thing I did was use my computer Bible program to print out all the Scripture texts on the subject. Scanning over those several pages of verses I was struck by the frequency with which the fear of God is linked to obeying Him. More than one-fourth of all the verses on my printout made such a connection.

For example, when the Israelites were about to enter the Promised Land, Moses said to them:

> *These are the commands, decrees and laws the LORD your God directed me to teach you to observe in the land that you are crossing the Jordan to possess, so that you, your children and their children after them may fear the LORD your God as long as you live by keeping all his decrees and commands that I give you, and so that you may enjoy long life. (Deuteronomy 6:1-2)*

Note the words, "so that you…may fear the LORD your God…by keeping all his decrees and commands." We fear the Lord by obeying Him. And it is a conscious obedience to *God's commands* as given in His Word that constitutes this godly fear.

The linkage of obedience to godly fear is continued throughout the Old Testament. Two sample passages will serve to show both sides of this obedience. Proverbs 8:13 says, "To fear the LORD is to hate evil," while Psalm 112:1 says, "Blessed is the man who fears the LORD, who finds great delight in his commands." Hating evil, on one hand, and delighting in God's commands, on the other, are both concrete expressions of the fear of God.

Scripture also draws a frequent connection between wickedness and the absence of fearing God. The first time the expression *fear of God* is used in the Bible, it's in this negative sense, when Abraham said, "There is surely no fear of God in this place" (Genesis 20:11). Later we read of the Amalekites who "had no fear of God" and therefore attacked the Israelites when they were weary and worn out (Deuteronomy 25:17-18). Quite obviously the same statements could be made about our society today. All the moral decadence we see is because people have no fear of God. God is seldom in their thoughts.

NOT FROM TERROR OR BONDAGE

Perhaps the best-known scripture linking the fear of God with obedience is Ecclesiastes 12:13: "Now all has been heard; here is the conclusion of the matter: Fear God and keep his commandments, for this is the whole duty of man."

The book of Ecclesiastes essentially teaches us how to live amid life's tensions, frustrations, and disappointments. Having covered a vast range of instructions, the "Teacher" (1:1; 12:9) sums up his findings: "Fear God and keep his commandments." Charles Bridges, a nineteenth-century Church of England minister, pointed out a contrast here between a "legal principle"—the fear of the consequences of disobeying God—and a spirit of "filial love" springing from an assured forgiveness of our sins through Christ:

> *Two short sentences sum up the whole—**Fear God, and keep his commandments.** The sentences are in their right order. **The fear of God** is the hidden principle of obedience. It is the work of the Spirit in the heart of the regenerate. It is not a legal principle of terror or bondage, but the genuine spirit of confidence—the delicate expression of filial love in the heart of the child of God—the holy fruit of forgiveness. Here we walk with our Father, humbly, acceptably, securely—looking not at an offended God with terror, but at a reconciled God with reverential love. All the gracious influences on the soul—cherished under the power of the Spirit—all flow out in godly **fear** towards him.*[1]

Though the fear of God does include a certain fear of incurring God's displeasure, the dominant element should be the filial love about which Charles Bridges speaks.

Yet we must not lose sight of the connection the Teacher draws between fearing God and keeping His commandments. Obedience is the fruit of the tree of which the fear of God is the root. We cannot rightly follow and obey God if we do not fear Him—we do not honor, reverence, and love Him.

OBEDIENCE OR MORALITY?

At this point we need to distinguish between obedience springing from the fear of God and mere human morality. There are many morally upright, decent people in our society who do not fear God. Their morality grows out of such things as family upbringing and perhaps church attendance, where they hear sermons urging them to be good and do their duty. Let me give you an example of this kind of morality. Here are three stanzas from an unknown author's poem that I clipped from a local business newspaper some time ago.

> *When you get what you want in your struggle for self*
> *And the world makes you a king for a day,*
> *Just go to the mirror and look at yourself,*
> *And see what THAT man has to say.*

For it isn't your father or mother or wife
Whose judgment upon you must pass;
The fellow whose verdict counts most in your life
Is the one staring back from the glass....

He's the fellow to please, never mind all the rest,
For he's with you clear up to the end,
And you've passed your most dangerous, difficult test
If the man in the glass is your friend.

The overall sentiment of the poem—the importance of personal integrity—is commendable. But it isn't an integrity that springs from the fear of God. In fact it's the "man in the glass"—not God—whom the author tells us we must satisfy. There's nothing about our obligation to God. It is mere human morality.

Sad to say, we Christians can lapse into this kind of morality—obedience to a certain moral lifestyle that has little to do with the fear of God. But morality does not qualify as biblical obedience unless it springs from the fear of God—from a reverential awe of who He is and what He has done for us.

YBH

You may be like the man who often wrote the letters "YBH" in the margins of the books he was reading. A friend, browsing through the man's library one day, noted the frequency of those letters and asked what they meant. "They stand for *Yes, but how?*" the man replied. "I agree with what the author is saying, but I need to know how to apply it."

Hopefully you agree with me that the fear of God should indeed be a foundational attitude in the life of a Christian. You're also persuaded that this fear, whether viewed as a complex set of emotions or a sustained attitude, should be *determinative* in the way we relate to God and to other people. And you agree that God is most worthy to be feared, both because of who He is and what He's done for us (as I explore more fully in *The Joy of Fearing God* and in *I Exalt You, O God: Encountering His Greatness in Your Private Worship*).

Now you want to know, "*How* do I grow in following God out of a proper sense of fear for him?"

The remainder of this book is intended to help you do this. In thirty-one daily readings, we'll look at specific steps for continuing to grow in following and fearing God as a life-long process.

ALREADY WITHIN YOU

The good news is that if you're a believer, God has *already* implanted in your heart the fear of Him—in principle. In Jeremiah 32:38-41 the Lord gives us a gracious promise:

> *They will be my people, and I will be their God. I will give them singleness of heart and action, so that they*

> *will always **fear** me for their own good and the good of*
> *their children after them. I will make an everlasting cove-*
> *nant with them: I will never stop doing good to them, and*
> *I will inspire them to **fear** me, so that they will never turn*
> *away from me. I will rejoice in doing them good and will*
> *assuredly plant them in this land with all my heart and*
> *soul.[2]*

Note the two references here to fearing God. First He says He will give us singleness of heart and action so that we'll always fear Him. Then He adds His promise to *inspire* us to fear Him, or as a more literal translation renders it, "I will put the fear of me in their hearts" (verse 40, RSV). God will do more than simply motivate us, as the word *inspire* might suggest; He will actually implant a principle of the fear of Him in our hearts. This is a part of regeneration when God gives us a new heart and puts His Spirit within us (Ezekiel 36:26-27).

If you've been born again and trust Christ as your Savior, you already have within you a basic foundation of the fear of God. In at least an elementary fashion, you already have that sense of "awe, reverence, honor, and worship" toward God that John Murray described. If you're a believer it is there, though it may be only a spark. It's only unbelievers who have "*no* fear of God before their eyes" (Romans 3:18).

FANNING THE SPARK

I've deliberately used a *spark* as a metaphor to picture this basic principle. I think for most of us it *is* only a spark at the beginning. Another reason I chose this word is because Paul told us to "fan into flame the gift of God, which is in you" (2 Timothy 1:6). Paul was actually referring to spiritual gifts, which God has given each of us. He wants us to develop our gifts, improving them so they'll be more useful. They are indeed gifts, but we have the responsibility to fan them into flame, to cause them to develop and mature.

We should also fan into flame the spark of the fear of God that He put within us at our new birth. That doesn't mean we do this on our own, apart from the Holy Spirit's help. It does mean that we're responsible to *grow* in fearing God. The initial kindling of the spark is solely the work of God; the flaring up of that spark into a flame is a combined effort: We ourselves work with the Holy Spirit, as enabled by His power.

This basic principle is also like a seed planted in the ground, which only the planter is aware of at first. It is God who has planted the seed of the fear of Him in our hearts, whether or not we have realized it. In this picture too we see the synergistic effort between God and ourselves. Paul said, "I planted the seed, Apollos watered it, but God made it grow. So neither he who plants nor he who waters is anything, but only God, who makes things grow" (1 Corinthians 3:6-7).

In the agricultural realm God has ordained that mankind be fully involved in the growth of crops, but He has reserved to Himself the principle of life, the ability to make things grow. It's the same way in the spiritual life. God ordains that we mature through personal diligence and effort, but He reserves to Himself the ability to make us grow. We're responsible to fan into flame the spark of the fear of God, but we're dependent on Him to make it happen.

SOMETHING TO PRAY FOR

This leads naturally to the first requirement for growing in the fear of God. We need to ask God to stimulate this growth within us. We can pray with David, "Give me an undivided heart, that I may fear your name" (Psalm 86:11).

An undivided heart denotes singleness of purpose, aim, and affections. This is what David prayed for. He recognized the tendency of his heart to be divided, to seek to serve two masters—himself and God—so he earnestly sought help from the Lord, that he might fear Him.

A lot of people in various pursuits—professional and businesspeople, athletes, farmers—have a singleness of heart and purpose, some to a fault. We sometimes call them "workaholics." But it's rare to find a Christian with an undivided heart. We're constantly pulled by the subtleties of the world and the desires of our sinful natures. So we need to pray that God will unite our hearts to fear His name.

This is where growth in the fear of God begins. God the Holy Spirit is the energizer of all spiritual motion in our lives. Without His work in our hearts, we cannot work. So our first step in growing in the fear of God is to pray for a heart single in purpose to that end.

Go back in Jeremiah 32:40 to God's promise to inspire us to fear Him and ask Him to do exactly that in your heart—not just plant the seed, but also cause it to grow. This should be a consistent prayer for each of us. I have six or eight verses of Scripture that I pray over almost every day, asking God to work out their truth in my life. One of them is Psalm 86:11: "Give me an undivided heart, that I may fear your name." I encourage you to make that scripture a part of your regular prayer times.

HEARING THE TRUTH

After prayer, the next ingredient for growth in fearing God is regular, consistent exposure of our minds and hearts to His Word. This exposure should involve reading it for ourselves, hearing it taught, and studying it for ourselves. All three of these methods of Scripture intake are involved.

In Deuteronomy 4:10 the Lord connects hearing His Word with learning to fear ("revere") Him: "Assemble the people before me to hear my words so that they may learn to revere me as long as they live in the land and may teach them to their children." So as we hear the Scriptures preached and taught we should pray that God will use them to stimulate our fear of Him.

When Saul of Tarsus fell down in fear before the risen, glorified Christ on the road to Damascus, he asked two questions: "Who are you, Lord?" and "What shall I do, Lord?" (Acts 22:8,10). These questions are helpful to ask as we hear God's Word taught: *Who are you, Lord?*—Lord, reveal Yourself to me in some aspect of Your greatness or holiness or wisdom or love. Show me more of who You really are. And, *What shall I do, Lord?*—how do You want me to apply and obey Your Word today in reverence to You?

God's Word is preached not to offer us helpful suggestions for improving our lives or making us feel good, but to teach us more of God, His person, His works, and His will for our daily lives. To that end, pray and listen attentively. Write down thoughts that are especially helpful for understanding or applying the scripture being expounded.

READING THE TRUTH

Another way we grow in the fear of the Lord is through regular reading of the Bible. Notice what each future king of Israel was commanded to do in Deuteronomy 17:18-19:

> *When he takes the throne of his kingdom, he is to write for himself on a scroll a copy of this law.... It is to be with him, and he is to read it all the days of his life so that he may*

learn to revere the LORD his God and follow carefully all
the words of this law and these decrees.

The king was to be a regular reader of God's law, specifically for the purpose of learning to fear the Lord and obey Him. What was true for Israel's kings should be true of us today. Regular, prayerful, personal exposure to Scripture is the most effective means of growing in the fear of God.

Whatever Bible-reading plan you use (and many are available today), I strongly urge you to include a regular reading through the Old Testament. Here we see God's holiness and sovereignty portrayed most vividly. Consider such a matter-of-fact report as this one:

That night the angel of the LORD went out and put to
death a hundred and eighty-five thousand men in the
Assyrian camp. When the people got up the next morn-
ing—there were all the dead bodies! (2 Kings 19:35)

Think of it: 185,000 men killed without ever "firing a shot"! You can hardly read this without being impressed with God's sovereignty over the world.

The Old Testament is filled with such stories. As you read these true accounts, stop and pray over them, asking God to use them to stir within you a deep sense of reverential awe.

Throughout these same Old Testament pages that reveal

God's sovereignty, we also discover His unfailing love and faithfulness to His people. (The Psalms alone contain some twenty-five references to the Lord's "unfailing love.") Even after He had punished them with exile, He still said to the Jews, "'When seventy years are completed for Babylon, I will come to you and fulfill my gracious promise to bring you back to this place. For I know the plans I have for you,' declares the LORD, 'plans to prosper you and not to harm you, plans to give you hope and a future'" (Jeremiah 29:10-11). God's love never failed even though He had to discipline the Jews severely for their persistent disobedience. I find it helpful to make notes in the margins of my Bible or in a separate notebook of what I learn from my reading about God's love and other attributes.

IN A GOSPEL ATMOSPHERE

As you move into the New Testament in your reading, pay close attention to the gospel—the mission of Christ in His life and death for us as an atoning sacrifice for our sins. We find this not just in the first four New Testament books, commonly called "the Gospels," but throughout the New Testament.

Consider, for example, the message of 2 Corinthians 5:21: "God made him who had no sin to be sin for us, so that in him we might become the righteousness of God." This verse essentially teaches us that God charged our sin to Christ and credited His righteousness to us. That's the gospel in a nutshell. Each time we read a passage such as this, we should stop and ponder God's amazing love for us as manifested in the Atonement.

"Godly fear," wrote John Bunyan,

flows from a sense of the love and kindness of God to the soul. Where there is no sense of hope of the kindness and mercy of God by Jesus Christ, there can be none of this fear, but rather wrath and despair, which produces a fear that is…devilish;…but godly fear flows from a sense of hope of mercy from God by Jesus Christ.[3]

Bunyan then quotes Psalm 130:3-4: "If you, O LORD, kept a record of sins, O Lord, who could stand? But with you there is forgiveness; therefore you are feared."

Notice the importance here, as an aspect of the fear of God, of His love drawing us to Him. The editor of Bunyan's works made this comment in a footnote: "The filial fear of God is most prevalent when the heart is impressed with a lively sense of the love of God manifested in Christ."[4]

With this in mind I cannot emphasize too strongly the importance of living our Christian lives each day in the atmosphere of the gospel. The gospel is not just for unbelievers. It is also for us, because we are still sinners—saved sinners to be sure, but still sinners in need of the daily assurance of God's forgiveness through Christ. As we experience His love through His forgiveness, our hearts are drawn to Him in this filial fear, and we stand amazed at His love.

GOING FOR DEPTH

Along with reading the Bible, we also need to *study* it. Bible reading gives us breadth, but Bible study gives us depth. Most people probably wouldn't grasp the message of 2 Corinthians 5:21 merely by reading through 2 Corinthians. Only as we begin to dig down into the meaning of a passage do we start mining Scripture's gold.

If you've never done serious Bible study, the idea may sound intimidating. For one thing, you don't know how to do it. You also don't know where to find regular time for it. A practical solution to both these problems is to get involved in a group Bible study where you can learn how to dig into the Scriptures and also benefit from the insights of others. A group Bible study also provides a measure of accountability that usually helps us to somehow find the time to prepare before meeting with the group.

A word of caution, however: All Bible study groups are not created equal. They vary from highly structured classroom approaches to informal gatherings in homes or restaurants. There's nothing wrong with an informal group, provided it promotes a serious attempt to grapple with the message of Scripture. You'll want to avoid a study where people merely share their subjective impressions of "what the passage says to me" apart from objective study of the text.

THE RIGHT ATTITUDE

Obviously some skills are needed in Bible study, and we'll seek to develop them if we're serious about growing in the fear of God. A number of good books are available today on *hermeneutics*—the principles and processes of biblical interpretation. You might ask your pastor or another mature Christian who is experienced in Bible study for a recommendation. Look for one that teaches objective study skills without promoting a particular doctrinal position.

More important than good study skills, however, is the right mental attitude. Proverbs 2:1-5 explains what it is:

> *My son, if you accept my words*
> *   and store up my commands within you,*
> *turning your ear to wisdom*
> *   and applying your heart to understanding,*
> *and if you call out for insight*
> *   and cry aloud for understanding,*
> *and if you look for it as for silver*
> *   and search for it as for hidden treasure,*
> *then you will understand the fear of the LORD*
> *   and find the knowledge of God.*

The right attitude here is characterized first by a *teachable* spirit. To "accept" Scripture's words suggests an attitude of openness to learn more and to be corrected. None of us possesses all the truth, and we don't fully understand the truth we have. So we always need to be willing to learn more or have our understanding corrected.

We need to avoid becoming like the Jews to whom Jesus said, "You diligently study the Scriptures because you think that by them you possess eternal life. These are the Scriptures that testify about me, yet you refuse to come to me to have life" (John 5:39-40). They were persistent in Bible study but they were not teachable. Their preconceived ideas about what Scripture taught kept them from being open to the message of Jesus.

DESPERATE DEPENDENCE

A proper mental attitude is also characterized by a spirit of *dependence.* This is expressed graphically in Proverbs 2:3 by the instruction to "call out for insight and cry aloud for understanding." There's almost a sense of desperateness conveyed. This isn't simply Jewish hyperbole. It squares with reality. The fact is we're desperately dependent. Consider the words of Jesus in Luke 10:21: "I praise you, Father, Lord of heaven and earth, because you have hidden these things from the wise and learned, and revealed them to little children. Yes, Father, for this was your good pleasure." The comments of Norval Geldenhuys on this passage help us see what Jesus was rejoicing about:

God in His wisdom, omnipotence and love has so arranged matters that insight is given into the redeeming truths of the kingdom not to those who are self-exalted and wise in their own esteem (as so many Pharisees and scribes were at that time), but to those (like His faithful disciples) who in childlike simplicity and humility feel their utter dependence on the Lord and accept without intellectual arrogance the truths revealed by God through Him. The contrast pointed by the Saviour is not that between "educated" and "uneducated" but between those who imagine themselves to be wise and sensible and want to test the Gospel truths by their own intellects and to pronounce judgment according to their self-formed ideas, and those who live under the profound impression that by their own insight and their own reasonings they are utterly powerless to understand the truths of God and to accept them.[5]

The attitude of those "who in childlike simplicity and humility feel their utter dependence on the Lord" goes hand in hand with a teachable spirit. If we're self-opinionated about what the Bible teaches, we'll be neither dependent nor teachable. Even those of us who want to be dependent and teachable can too often give lip service to those qualities while actually approaching Bible study in the strength of our own intellect. We need to ask God to help us live, in the words of Geldenhuys, under the profound impression that by our own insight and reasoning we're utterly powerless to understand and accept God's truths.

LOOKING FOR TREASURE

The third characteristic of a right attitude toward Bible study is *diligence.* This is expressed in Proverbs 2:2,4 by the phrases "applying your heart to understanding," "look[ing] for it as for silver," and "search[ing] for it as for hidden treasure." Prayer cannot take the place of diligence. We depend upon the Holy Spirit, but He answers our prayers and enlightens us as we diligently apply our minds to the text of Scripture. The idea of looking for silver and searching for hidden treasure suggests that Scripture truth is valuable and worth digging out, but the digging is indeed labor.

What is the result of such open-minded, prayerful, and diligent Bible study? Solomon said in Proverbs 2:5, "You will understand the fear of the LORD and find the knowledge of God." Once again we see that consistent exposure to Scripture is the path to growing in the fear of God. The more we know God, the more we will fear Him. The more we see His majesty, sovereignty, and love, the more we will stand in awe of Him.

Listen again to John Bunyan:

> *The fear of God flows from...a sound impression that the word of God makes on our souls; for without an impress of the Word, there is no fear of God. Hence it is said that God*

gave to Israel good laws, statutes and judgments that they might learn them, and in learning them, learn to fear the Lord their God....For as [to the extent] a man drinks good doctrine into his soul, so [to that extent] he fears God. If he drinks in much, he fears Him greatly; if he drinks in but little, he fears Him but little; if he drinks it not at all, he fears Him not at all.[6]

YOUR PRIVATE WORSHIP

This book is presented as a companion and guide to your private worship and is arranged in the same format as *I Exalt You, O God*. As I pointed out in that book as well as in *The Joy of Fearing God*, both private and corporate worship—that which we do individually and that which we do with other believers—are taught in Scripture, and the vitality and genuineness of corporate worship is to a large degree dependent upon the vitality of our individual private worship.

To grow in following God and fearing Him in our private worship, we must ask ourselves some hard questions:

1. Have I presented myself and all that I have to God as a living sacrifice, so that my way of life is one of worship?

2. Do I take time daily to worship God privately and to thank Him for all His blessings to me?

3. Is there some "cherished" sin, some practice I'm unwilling to give up, that hinders my worship?

4. Do I seek to enter wholeheartedly and "in spirit and truth" into worship? Or do I simply go through the motions without really worshiping?

None of us will score perfectly on these questions. That is not their intent. Rather, they're designed to help us honestly assess ourselves and pinpoint areas of our lives that need improvement. Only then, and as we take steps to improve, will this book be of benefit to us.

Part I

I Will Follow You, O God...

LIVING ALL OF LIFE IN YOUR
CONSCIOUS PRESENCE

You will fill me with joy in your presence.

PSALM 16:11

God is our refuge and strength, an ever-present help in trouble.

PSALM 46:1

Where can I go from your Spirit?
Where can I flee from your presence?

PSALM 139:7

D a y   1

HE IS HERE

Several years ago a Christian magazine published an anonymous article by a Christian leader recounting his fall into pornography. It all began when, alone in a hotel room in a distant city, he saw an advertisement for an exotic dancer at a local nightclub. Rationalizing to himself that to be an effective Christian leader he had to experience all of life, he was soon on his way to the show.

But it didn't stop there. He was hooked, and for the next five years he fought a desperate battle with extreme sexual lust.

Suppose that instead of his being alone, the man's wife or perhaps an elder from his church had been with him that night. Would he have gone to the show? Of course not.

But the fact is *God* was with him. God was there looking with indignation on that performance designed to excite men's lust. God was there looking with grief on His erring child. As He says of His people in Jeremiah 16:17, "My eyes are on all their ways; they are not hidden from me, nor is their sin concealed from my eyes."

A God-fearing person lives all of life in the conscious presence of God. I use the phrase *conscious presence* deliberately. The truth is, we live at all times in the presence of God whether we're aware of it or not. We can say with David,

> *Where can I go from your Spirit?*
> > *Where can I flee from your presence?*
> *If I go up to the heavens, you are there;*
> > *if I make my bed in the depths, you are there.*
> *If I rise on the wings of the dawn,*
> > *if I settle on the far side of the sea,*
> *even there your hand will guide me,*
> > *your right hand will hold me fast. (Psalm 139:7-10)*

As a God-fearing man, David was keenly aware of never being absent from God's all-pervasive presence. Neither the height of the heavens nor the depth of the earth nor the farthest boundaries of the sea could provide an escape from God. Wherever David went, God was there beholding all he did.

To help us understand this, the Bible teaches both the *immensity* and the *omnipresence* of God. These two descriptive terms are related but distinct, as theologian A. A. Hodge points out:

> *The immensity of God is the phrase used to express the fact*
> *that God is infinite in his relation to space, i.e., that the*

*entire indivisible essence of God is at every moment of time
contemporaneously present to every point of infinite
space....*

*Omnipresence characterizes the relation of God to his
creatures as they severally occupy their several positions in
space.*[7]

Perhaps the two terms are best understood by use of
human analogy. As I write, I'm sitting behind my desk. By
reaching forward with my arm I can barely touch the front
of it. But I can't be both behind and in front of my desk at
the same time. God, however, is both behind my desk and in
front of it at all times, not by extension of His "arms," so to
speak, but with His entire being. He is in fact everywhere
present in my study, in our house, and in the entire universe.
Even on the most distant star in the universe, God is there in
His indivisible essence just as much as He is in my study.
That is God's immensity.

Solomon acknowledged God's immensity in his dedica-
tion prayer for the temple: "But will God really dwell on
earth? The heavens, even the highest heaven, cannot contain
you. How much less this temple I have built!" (1 Kings 8:27).

God's omnipresence arises obviously from His immen-
sity and refers to His continuous presence *with each of us*.
This is what David was acknowledging to God in Psalm 139.
Wherever we are, "You are there." God is with me in my

study and with my wife in the kitchen at the same time. When I travel to a distant city, God is just as much with my wife back home as He is with me on my trip. He is present with my Chinese Christian brother on the other side of the world just as much as He's with me in Colorado. Even if we could travel in a spaceship to that most distant star, God would be there with us.

Jeremiah 23:23-24 speaks to both God's immensity and His omnipresence:

> "Am I only a God nearby,"
>> declares the LORD,
> "and not a God far away?
> Can anyone hide in secret places
>> so that I cannot see him?"
>> declares the LORD.
> "Do not I fill heaven and earth?"
>> declares the LORD.

Yes, Lord, You truly do fill heaven and earth, and indeed the reach of Your presence far exceeds even that, since "the heavens, even the highest heaven, cannot contain you." For all this I praise and worship You today. "Be exalted, O God, above the heavens, and let your glory be over all the earth." Jeremiah 23:24; 1 Kings 8:27; Psalm 108:5

*Because You are **everywhere**, I can always know that You are **here**! My longing is to live in the full awareness of this reality and to know the blessing that comes from it. "Blessed are those who have learned to acclaim you, who walk in the light of your presence, O LORD."* Psalm 89:15

And because of the salvation You have granted me through the death of Your Son, Jesus Christ, I look forward to the indescribable experience of being with You for all eternity. "You will fill me with joy in your presence, with eternal pleasures at your right hand." Psalm 16:11

IN HIS SIGHT
AND COMPANY

The omnipresence of God means that we are never out of His presence and His all-seeing eye. We can hide from one another—or hide our activities from each other—but never from God. As Proverbs 15:3 says, "The eyes of the LORD are everywhere, keeping watch on the wicked and the good."

A God-fearing person is continually aware that wherever he or she goes, God is there. Such a consciousness of God's presence should obviously affect our conduct. As J. I. Packer has written, "Living becomes an awesome business when you realize that you spend every moment of your life in the sight and company of an omniscient, omnipresent Creator."[8]

Which of us isn't guilty sometimes of disregarding God's constant presence? If you've ever slowed down to the speed limit at the sight of a highway patrol car, you were driving without the conscious presence of God. God, not the state trooper, should be our highway patrolman, because God is always with us. A God-fearing person should be the same at all times, knowing we live every moment of our lives in His presence. We need to establish the habit, though, of constantly being aware of this fact.

David was keenly aware of God's constant presence. "You know when I sit and when I rise," he acknowledged. "You discern my going out and my lying down; you are familiar with all my ways" (Psalm 139:2-3). The God who created the universe and keeps the stars in their courses takes note of every move we make. He observes our slightest sideward glance and hears our every whispered word.

The person who follows God in godly fear—who properly relates to Him with awe, reverence, honor, and worship—will be conscious that God is aware of every minute detail, every mundane activity in his or her life. Such awareness serves as a check on temptation to sin. This doesn't mean living in constant fear that God is going to "get us." It does mean that because we're aware of His all-seeing eye and all-hearing ear, we live in a way that pleases Him as He sees what we do and hears what we say.

Paul's instruction to slaves in Colossians 3:22-25 was to obey whether or not they were under the eye of their master. The reality is that God is present whether the master is there or not. Applying this principle to today's working world, we see that the Christian is always to work not just to win his or her employer's favor, but as if working for the Lord and under His watchful eye. This means we don't steal time, for example, in extra-long coffee or lunch breaks, or do shoddy work because no supervisor is there to observe us. It means that we accurately report business expenses because it is God, not just the controller's department, who audits our reports.

In the same manner, Paul's instructions to masters to provide their slaves "with what is right and fair" was based on the fact that masters also "have a Master in heaven" (Colossians 4:1). God was watching over their treatment of slaves with His all-seeing eye.

The truth, then, is that every interaction we have with another person is performed in the presence of God.

In Leviticus 19:14 is a rather intriguing warning regarding physically disabled people: "Do not curse the deaf or put a stumbling block in front of the blind, but fear your God. I am the LORD." I can't imagine the necessity for such a warning in the respectful Jewish culture, but obviously God knew it was needed. In our society today I can imagine some mischievous and immature teenagers gleefully cursing or insulting a deaf person or even deliberately setting up an obstacle for a blind person to stumble over.

In both cases the biblical warning is couched in terms of the fear of God. The deaf person can't hear himself being cursed, but God hears. The blind person can see neither the stumbling block nor whoever put it in his way, but God sees.

Undoubtedly in this context, the most prominent aspect of the fear of God is an actual fear of His retributive justice.

Implied in all these instructions and warnings is an underlying principle of integrity. We should never take advantage of anyone: the poor, the disabled, the buyer or seller, our employer or employees. Rather, in all our affairs of life and our interactions with other people, we should always be conscious of His all-pervasive presence, His all-seeing eye, and His all-hearing ear. This is where integrity actually begins—living all of life in the conscious awareness of God's constant presence.

Are there recurring events or activities in your life in which you need to make a special effort to practice the awareness of His presence as a restraint against temptation?

Mighty God, my Master in heaven, I thank You that Your loving eyes never leave me, that I will spend every moment of this day and every day in Your sight and in Your company. Wherever I go, whatever move I make, I can always know what David knew: "You are there…you are there." Psalm 139:8

At this moment, loving Lord, the eyes of my heart are on You, knowing that Yours are on me. I celebrate Your perfect knowledge of me. I rejoice that I can never escape Your Spirit or outrun Your presence, even if I tried. Psalm 139:7

I praise You that today Your guidance and power are available to help me please You in everything I do and say, and in my every interaction with other people. I praise You for Your own perfect integrity, and I thank You for Your promise to guide me in integrity, as I remember Your all-pervasive strength, Your all-seeing eye, and Your all-hearing ear. "May integrity and uprightness protect me, because my hope is in you." Psalm 25:21

*Before You, O God, I acknowledge that by my own insight and reasoning I am utterly powerless to accept or even understand the truth of Your continuing presence, or indeed to comprehend any of Your truth; I depend totally on **Your** enlightenment and teaching through the gift of Your Spirit, and for these I ask: "Teach me your way, O LORD, and I will walk in your truth; give me an undivided heart, that I may fear your name."* Psalm 86:11

Day 3

Our Every Thought in Exact Detail

God not only sees and hears all we do or say; He even knows our thoughts. "You perceive my thoughts from afar," David said. "Before a word is on my tongue you know it completely, O LORD" (Psalm 139:2,4). Psalm 44:21 also tells us that God "knows the secrets of the heart." And in Jeremiah 17:10, God says, "I the LORD search the heart and examine the mind."

Therefore to live in God's conscious presence means that we also live in the awareness that God knows our every thought. All of us have thoughts that we would be ashamed for other people to know. We entertain thoughts of jealousy, covetousness, envy, resentment, and lust. We have critical thoughts about another person's dress or speech or manner-isms. We mentally argue with people, or in our minds tell off someone in a way we wouldn't dare verbalize. As someone has humorously said, if all our thoughts for the past week were projected on a screen for others to see, we'd have to leave town.

But our thoughts are no joking matter to God. Thoughts

that we would be ashamed to share with our spouse or closest friend are all fully known to God. He knows them in the exact same detail that we think them. As Hebrews 4:13 so forcefully states, "Nothing in all creation is hidden from God's sight. Everything is uncovered and laid bare before the eyes of him *to whom we must give account.*" This passage suggests that we'll have to give an account to God for every sinful thought.

Jesus said, "I tell you that men will have to give account on the day of judgment for every careless word they have spoken" (Matthew 12:36). It is sobering to realize that this same accountability holds true not only for our words and deeds but even for our thoughts.

Since God knows our every thought in exact detail, we please Him by seeking to control our thought life in the same way we regulate our conduct. If we wouldn't go to the nightclub to see the exotic dancer, we don't allow thoughts of that nature to lodge in our minds. If we wouldn't murder, then we don't harbor thoughts of anger and resentment toward another person. It's true that anger is not as serious as murder, nor lustful thoughts as serious as adultery, but Jesus makes it clear that our thoughts and heart attitudes are judged by God just as much as our actions (see Matthew 5:21-22,27-28).

Solomon warned us, "Above all else, guard your heart, for it is the wellspring of life" (Proverbs 4:23). The Hebrew word for *heart* generally refers to our entire conscious person—our reasoning, understanding, emotions, conscience, and will. You can readily see, however, that all those internal activities are carried out in the realm of our thoughts. So basically Solomon was warning us to guard our thoughts.

Paul said, "We take captive every thought to make it obedient to Christ" (2 Corinthians 10:5). Although the context indicates he was referring to the thoughts of his opponents at Corinth, it still is a worthy objective for us regarding our own thought lives. We need to be as obedient in our thoughts as in our actions.

Controlling our thought life has two sides to it. We must both deal with negative, sinful thoughts and seek to fill our minds with positive, godly thoughts. Paul's description of godly thought patterns in Philippians 4:8 is a good model: "Finally, brothers, whatever is true, whatever is noble, whatever is right, whatever is pure, whatever is lovely, whatever is admirable—if anything is excellent or praiseworthy—think about such things."

Using Paul's list we can ask the following questions to evaluate our thoughts:

- *Is it true?* Are my thoughts about a person or a situation really accurate? Am I ascribing a sinful motive to someone without actually knowing the person's motive?

- *Is it noble?* Does this thought express the highest Christian ideals? Does it put another person in the best possible light?
- *Is it right?* Is it just and fair toward other people? Or does it tend to injure or defraud (even in our minds) another person's reputation?
- *Is it pure?* Is it morally and sexually pure?
- *Is it lovely?* Is it attractive and amiable? Do our thought patterns make us easy for others to deal with?
- *Is it admirable?* Would this thought receive the esteem of others if it were known?
- *Is it excellent or praiseworthy?* Is it commendable even to my own conscience?

Paul was obviously setting before us the highest standard for our thought life. I confess to squirming a bit even as I wrote out those questions. My thought patterns, I'm afraid, often fall short of Paul's ideal.

But dare we settle for any lower standard when we think all our thoughts in the presence of God? Even though we'll continually fall short, we must seek to make every thought obedient to Christ. And because we need the Lord's help, we do well to pray with David, "May the words of my mouth and the meditation of my heart be pleasing in your sight, O LORD, my Rock and my Redeemer" (Psalm 19:14).

As you review Paul's description of a positive thought life in Philippians 4:8, is the Holy Spirit specifically speaking to you about one of those qualities? If so, what do you need to do to change?

*How awesome You are, Mighty God! In Your presence today I acknowledge that "the eyes of the LORD are everywhere, keeping watch on the wicked and the good." I know that Your eyes today are not only on everything I do and say but also on everything I think and feel. For "nothing in all creation is hidden from God's sight"; before Your eyes "everything is uncovered and laid bare," and therefore to You I must give account.*Proverbs 15:3; Hebrews 4:13

You are worthy, Holy God, to judge all my innermost thoughts, for all Your own thoughts and motives and intentions are perfectly true and noble and right and pure and lovely and admirable and excellent and worthy of praise! "Praise the LORD, O my soul; all my inmost being, praise his holy name."
Philippians 4:8; Psalm 103:1

My longing, Lord God, is to have my own thoughts more closely reflect Yours, and so today I lift up David's prayer as my own: "May the words of my mouth and the meditation of my heart be pleasing in your sight, O LORD, my Rock and my Redeemer." Psalm 19:14

HE KNOWS ALL OUR MOTIVES

God's knowledge of us penetrates even deeper than our thoughts. It reaches to our motives, to why we do what we do. "The LORD searches every heart and understands every motive behind the thoughts" (1 Chronicles 28:9). We sometimes do the right thing for the wrong reason, or perhaps a combination of right and wrong reasons. We sincerely want to help someone or contribute to some worthy objective, but we also want to look good in the process.

Sometimes we're not even aware of our mixed motives, but God sees motives that we don't. Paul wrote,

> *My conscience is clear, but that does not make me innocent. It is the Lord who judges me. Therefore judge nothing before the appointed time; wait till the Lord comes. He will bring to light what is hidden in darkness and will expose the motives of men's hearts. At that time each will receive his praise from God. (1 Corinthians 4:4-5)*

Paul's conscience was clear, but he recognized that he might have hidden motives of which even he was not aware. This fact shouldn't make us introspective, always questioning whether our motives are right and pure. But it *should* cause us to recognize that our motives often are mixed at best. When we recognize a wrong motive we should confess it, claiming the cleansing blood of Christ (1 John 1:7). And we should ask God to make us aware of wrong motives we don't see.

The important thing to realize is that everything about us—not only every word and action but also every thought and motive—lies before God as an open book. To reverently follow God means living in this continual awareness of His presence and knowledge.

Today, O Lord, I worship You with gladness. I praise You, all-seeing God, that the time is coming when You "will bring to light what is hidden in darkness and will expose the motives of men's hearts." I praise You that even now my every thought and motive is always before You as an open book. You search my heart and understand every motive behind my every thought.
Psalm 100:2; 1 Corinthians 4:5; 1 Chronicles 28:9

You are entirely worthy to possess this perfect knowledge about me, because You created me and own me, and You are perfectly holy and righteous. You are my Lord, my Holy One, my Creator, and my King.^{Isaiah 43:15}

I also praise You today as my Savior. Thank You that whenever I recognize my wrong and inadequate motives, I can come to You in confession and be cleansed through Your Son, Jesus Christ. In His name, and by the power of His blood and His resurrection, I worship You, O faithful and righteous Lord.
1 John 1:9

HE ALWAYS HOLDS
OUR HAND

The fact that we live in the constant presence of God should be not only sobering but also encouraging to us. Note the transition David makes in Psalm 139. In verse 7 he acknowledges that he cannot *flee* from God's presence. In verse 10 he speaks of God's right hand holding him fast, like a parent tightly gripping the hand of a small child both to guide him and to protect him from danger. David has moved from God's *watchful presence* to consideration of His *protecting presence.*

When our children were small and we were in a crowd or crossing a busy street, I wasn't satisfied for them to hold my hand. I wanted to hold theirs. This was reinforced when I once had the frightening experience of losing our three-year-old daughter in the supermarket. I knew that in the jostling of a crowd my son or daughter could easily lose my hand, or while crossing a street they might let go to run across. So I held on tightly. Of course it was most often a mutual thing. They were insecure enough to cling as tightly to my hand as I gripped theirs.

That's a picture of God's way with us. He is pleased when we cling to His hand, so to speak, in dependence upon Him. But whether we cling to Him or not, He grips our hand. As David said, "Your right hand will hold me fast" (Psalm 139:10).

We see this picture again in Psalm 73, where Asaph wrote, "Yet I am always with you; you hold me by my right hand" (verse 23). The context of that verse is worth noting to fully appreciate what Asaph was saying. Early in the psalm Asaph was struggling with an apparent injustice of God: The wicked always seemed to be prospering. "This is what the wicked are like," Asaph concluded, "always carefree, they increase in wealth" (verse 12).

In contrast Asaph looked at himself: "Surely in vain have I kept my heart pure; in vain have I washed my hands in innocence" (verse 13). It seemed to him that the godly were worse off than the wicked. Then Asaph came to his senses and confessed, "When my heart was grieved and my spirit embittered, I was senseless and ignorant; I was a brute beast before you" (verses 21-22).

Immediately after this confession, Asaph acknowledged God's faithfulness and His constant care. He realized God always held him by his right hand even when circumstances tempted him to think otherwise.

If we truly follow God with the right sense of reverence and honor for Him, we, too, will confess with Asaph that God always holds us by our hand—even when it seems He is not.

The truth of God's continuous protecting presence is taught throughout Scripture. As Moses was preparing to turn over to Joshua his role of leading Israel, he said to Joshua and the people, "The LORD himself goes before you and will be with you; he will never leave you nor forsake you. Do not be afraid; do not be discouraged" (Deuteronomy 31:8). The Lord would go before them and be with them. He would never leave them nor forsake them.

This same promise is repeated in one form or another in several places in the Old Testament. (See Genesis 28:15; Deuteronomy 31:6,8; Joshua 1:5; and 1 Chronicles 28:20.) The writer of Hebrews also picks it up when he says, "Keep your lives free from the love of money and be content with what you have, because God has said, 'Never will I leave you; never will I forsake you'" (13:5).

Father in heaven, I worship You today as I enter Your holy presence by the body and blood of Your Holy Son, Jesus Christ.
Hebrews 10:19-20

I welcome and glory in the truth that "I am always with you; you hold me by my right hand." I welcome and glory in

*the truth that You will never leave me or forsake me. I welcome
and glory in the truth that wherever I go, "your right hand
will hold me fast."* Psalm 73:23; Deuteronomy 31:8; Psalm 139:10

*Lord God, in Your promise to Your people I hear Your
heart of love and faithfulness and constant care: "For I am the
LORD, your God, who takes hold of your right hand and says
to you, Do not fear; I will help you." In gratitude I freely offer
You my hand to hold.* Isaiah 41:13

*Your close presence is truly my desire, O God. "As the deer
pants for streams of water, so my soul pants for you, O God.
My soul thirsts for God, for the living God." I feel this way
because I've known before what it means when You "fill me
with joy in your presence," and I ask You to do this again.*
Psalms 42:1-2; 16:11

OUR REASON FOR NOT BEING AFRAID

Closely associated with the promise of God's continuous protective presence is His command of encouragement, "Don't be afraid." I was amazed when I pulled up on my computer screen verses with the phrase "don't [or do not] be afraid." This refrain occurs throughout the Bible from Genesis 15:1 to Revelation 2:10. It is of course because God is always with us that we should not be afraid. For example, in 1 Chronicles 28:20, David said to Solomon, "Do not be afraid or discouraged, for the LORD God, my God, is with you." The little child is not afraid as long as his mommy or daddy grips his hand. It's when he somehow gets separated from them that he becomes afraid.

God, however, is always with us. It's impossible for one of His children to become separated from Him, whatever our perception may be. David apparently felt separated from God on numerous occasions. In Psalm 10:1 he complained that God hides Himself in times of trouble. In Psalm 13:1 he asked, "How long, O LORD? Will you forget me forever?" In Psalm 31:22 he exclaimed, "I am cut off from your sight!" But then he added, "Yet you heard my cry for mercy when I called to you for help." God is always with us, holding our hand and saying, "Don't be afraid," even when we don't perceive His presence.

My wife and I signed up for a study program in Israel, the fulfillment of a twenty-year dream of mine. We were to fly from Denver to Atlanta, where we would meet the other members of our party and then travel as a group to Tel Aviv. There we would be met by our study leader and a bus to take us to our first destination in southern Israel.

I carefully arranged our flight schedule so we would arrive in Atlanta four hours before our transatlantic flight departed—plenty of time, I thought, to allow for any delay in the Denver-Atlanta flight. I was wrong. The airplane in Denver had a mechanical problem. We tried to get on another flight but were unsuccessful. There was nothing to do but wait for the plane's repair. We finally taxied out to the runway and started to take off, only to develop another mechanical problem. By the time this, too, was repaired, we had lost our four hours.

During that time of waiting in Denver, two passages of Scripture kept going through my mind. The first was Ecclesiastes 7:13: "Consider what God has done: Who can straighten what he has made crooked?" I knew God was sovereignly in control of our schedule, and it was becoming apparent to me that He was thwarting or "making crooked" our plan to be on the flight to Israel with our group.

The second passage of Scripture was the promise in Hebrews 13:5: "Never will I leave you; never will I forsake you." It seemed as if God was saying to me through those scriptures, "I'm not going to let you make that flight in Atlanta, however hard you try. You cannot straighten what I have made crooked. But don't be afraid; I will not forsake you. Even though you'll arrive in Israel long after your group does, I will not leave you stranded."

I needed that reassurance. As it turned out, God did thwart our plans. We missed our flight to Israel and had to wait twenty-four hours for the next one. It was a disappointment to realize we would miss the first day of our study program, but my main concern was what we would do when we landed in Israel by ourselves. We would arrive about 6:00 P.M.; where would we stay that first night? How would we locate our group, and how would we get to where they were? I know these are not earthshaking concerns, but I'm not the adventuresome type. To say the least, I was struggling with anxiety.

Through the airline I sent a message ahead to Tel Aviv telling of our delay, but I had no assurance it would get through (especially since a previous message from Denver to Atlanta had not).

We finally landed in Israel and walked out of the Tel Aviv airport into a huge crowd of people waiting to meet other passengers. What would we do? At that moment my wife spotted a man holding a sign that read, "Mr. and Mrs. Bridges." He loaded us into a Volkswagen van and drove us about four or five hours into the desert to where our study group was spending the night. It was midnight and everyone was in bed, but we managed to find our assigned room. At last we had arrived. God had not left us stranded in Tel Aviv. He had not forsaken us.

I realize our little episode pales in comparison with the major crises others face, such as losing your job when you're the primary or only source of family income. It pales in comparison with the death of my first wife after a seventeen-month bout with cancer. But whether we're facing a major or minor crisis in our lives, God's promise is the same. He will never leave us; He will never forsake us. This is the assurance we can have as we learn to live in the protective presence of God.

Are there recurring events or activities in your life in which you need to make a special effort to practice the awareness of His presence as an encouragement that God's protective presence is with you?

∾

*Thank You, loving and mighty God, for Your perfect protection of me. This I know: "that God is for me"; and since **You** are for me, who can be against me? Therefore, "in God I trust; I will not be afraid."* Psalm 56:9,11; Romans 8:31

You, O Lord, are my Shepherd, and I shall never be in want. "Even though I walk through the valley of the shadow of death, I will fear no evil, for you are with me; your rod and your staff, they comfort me.... Surely goodness and love will follow me all the days of my life, and I will dwell in the house of the LORD forever." Psalm 23

*I praise you, O Lord, and I testify, "Surely God is my salvation; I will trust and not be afraid. The LORD, the LORD, is my strength and my song; he has become my salvation." "I sought the LORD, and he answered **me**; he delivered **me** from all my fears.* Isaiah 12:2; Psalm 34:4

SEEING ALL, HE STILL LOVES US

There's still more good news about God's constant presence with us and His knowledge of us. Despite all He sees and knows of our sin, He still loves us. When He chose us in Christ even before the creation of the world (Ephesians 1:4), He knew even then about all our sinful ways, all our unholy thoughts, all our unkind words and self-centered motives. He chose us not because He foresaw that we would be good, but because of His own sovereign love for us.

When God the Father sent His Son to be the atoning sacrifice for our sins, He laid on Him the iniquity of us all (Isaiah 53:6). Christ bore all our sins on the cross. Because of that, the apostle Paul could write, "He forgave us all our sins" (Colossians 2:13), and "Blessed is the man whose sin the Lord will never count against him" (Romans 4:8). Despite all the sin God sees in our lives, He has cleansed us with the blood of Christ and clothed us with His righteousness. We are still sinners, but we are forgiven sinners.

Because of this we can be absolutely honest before God. We should be, because He knows all about us anyway. But too often, because of a sense of guilt, we try in some way to hide our sin from God by rationalizing it or seeking in some way to justify or excuse it. We're like the little boy protesting, "But he hit me first!"

We can also be brutally honest with ourselves. However ugly our sin may be, we know that it is covered by the blood of Christ. If we have spoken critically or slanderously about someone, we can admit it, calling it exactly what it is. If we have padded our expense account report, we can face the fact that we have effectively stolen from our employer.

David had learned the freedom of knowing how God knew all about him and still loved him. Because of this he willingly asked God to search his heart for any offensive ways in him (Psalm 139:23-24). If you and I learn this freedom, we, too, can ask God to search our hearts. We can ask Him to reveal sin that we aren't even aware of, sins such as selfishness, pride, and stubbornness. It's painful to have such sins brought to light, but we must see them before we can repent of them and deal with them.

People who rightly follow God live their lives in the conscious presence of God. They act, speak, and think in the continual awareness that He sees all their actions, hears all their words, and knows all their thoughts. On the one hand, this has a sobering and restraining influence on them to keep them from sin, even in their thoughts, On the other hand, they have the joy of knowing that even though God knows all about their sin, He has forgiven them through Christ and accepts them through His merit.

They're grateful for both the restraining influence and the assurance of forgiveness that comes from knowing they live constantly in His presence. And in this they experience joy.

How consistently do you practice the conscious awareness of God's presence? Can you think of situations where you would have acted differently if you had been practicing the presence of God?

What steps do you intend to take to grow in your practice of the conscious presence of God?

You know me so completely and yet also You love me so completely! How amazing is Your love! Show me more and more how awesome and amazing Your love really is. "For great is your love, higher than the heavens; your faithfulness reaches to the skies." Psalm 108:4

You showed me Your great love by sending Your one and only Son into the world as an atoning sacrifice for my sins, that through Him I might live. This is perfect love, awesome love, astounding love. 1 John 4:8-10

You have not treated me as my sins deserve or repaid me according to my iniquities. You are "rich in mercy," and in

Christ, through His blood, You have lavished upon me the riches of Your forgiveness and grace. Thank You, loving Father! "The Lord our God is merciful and forgiving, even though we have rebelled against him." Psalm 103:10; Ephesians 2:4; 1:7-8; Daniel 9:9

"How priceless is your unfailing love!" "I will praise you, O Lord my God, with all my heart; I will glorify your name forever. For great is your love toward me; you have delivered me from the depths of the grave." Psalms 36:7; 86:12-13

"To you, O Lord, I lift up my soul. You are forgiving and good, O Lord, abounding in love to all who call to you." "To your name be the glory, because of your love and faithfulness." Psalms 86:4-5; 115:1

Because of Your great love that has purchased forgiveness of my sins through the sacrifice of Jesus Christ, I can be totally honest with You and totally honest with myself. Therefore today I lift up David's prayer as my own: "Search me, O God, and know my heart; test me and know my anxious thoughts. See if there is any offensive way in me, and lead me in the way everlasting." Psalm 139:23-24

Meeting God

GREAT GOD,

In public and private, in sanctuary and home,

   may my life be steeped in prayer,

      filled with the spirit of grace and supplication,

        each prayer perfumed with the incense of atoning blood.

Help me, defend me, until from praying ground

I pass to the realm of unceasing praise.

Urged by my need,

Invited by thy promises,

Called by thy Spirit,

I enter thy presence, worshipping thee with godly fear,

          awed by thy majesty, greatness, glory,

            but encouraged by thy love.

I am all poverty as well as all guilt,

      having nothing of my own with which to repay thee,

But I bring Jesus to thee in the arms of faith,

      pleading his righteousness to offset my iniquities,

      rejoicing that he will weigh down the scales for me,

      and satisfy thy justice.

I bless thee that great sin draws out great grace,

        that, although the least sin deserves infinite

        punishment

        because done against an infinite God,

yet there is mercy for me,

for where guilt is most terrible,

there thy mercy in Christ is most free and deep.

Bless me by revealing to me more of his saving merits,

by causing thy goodness to pass before me,

by speaking peace to my contrite heart;

Strengthen me to give thee no rest

until Christ shall reign supreme within me,

in every thought, word, and deed,

in a faith that purifies the heart,

overcomes the world, works by love,

fastens me to thee, and ever clings to the cross.

—THE VALLEY OF VISION

Part II

I Will Follow You, O God...

TRULY DEPENDING ON YOU FOR EVERYTHING

In him all things hold together.

COLOSSIANS 1:17

My salvation and my honor depend on God;
he is my mighty rock, my refuge.

PSALM 62:7

My flesh and my heart may fail,
but God is the strength of my heart
and my portion forever.

PSALM 73:26

FOR LIFE AND BREATH
AND EVERYTHING

Independence and self-sufficiency are hallmarks of our civilization. Children are trained from infancy to make it on their own. The childhood story of the little locomotive that chugged up the mountain saying, "I think I can, I think I can" is one illustration of how we seek to develop self-reliance and determination even in preschoolers. Later on, high-school athletes are urged to reach deep within themselves to find the courage and fortitude to win their games. Adults are told that if we simply believe in ourselves, we can become whatever we want to be. Even in the spiritual realm, a prominent physician said, "I have great belief in spiritual strength, but spiritual strength, to me, comes from within."

This independence is to some extent inbred in human nature. I remember one of our children, still in the highchair stage, refusing to be helped by stubbornly asserting, "Me can do it!" Of course we want children to grow up with a reasonable degree of self-confidence and a realization that they can develop the necessary skills and maturity to make it on their own in life. At the same time, however, we should realize that God wants us to learn the truth of our absolute dependence on Him.

We have seen that a person who truly follows God— rightly relating to Him with awe, reverence, honor, and worship—will live all of life in the conscious presence of God. Another characteristic of such a person is that *he or she lives all of life in conscious dependence on God.* Again I use the word *conscious* deliberately, because whether we realize it or not, we're actually dependent upon God every moment of our lives.

John Murray described this characteristic well: "God is constantly in the center of our thought and apprehension, and life is characterized by the all-pervasive consciousness of dependence upon him and responsibility to him."[9] This attitude of absolute dependence on God is not one to be temporarily assumed, as in a time of crisis, but is to be sustained through all the routine activities of life, both spiritual and temporal. We need to cultivate a spirit of dependence on God just as much in driving to church as in teaching a Sunday school class once we get there.

This absolute dependence upon God for everything is taught clearly in Acts 17:25, where Paul told the Athenians that God "is not served by human hands, as if he needed anything, because he himself gives all men life and breath and everything else."

We're dependent upon God for life itself. David recognized this when he said, "My times are in your hands" (Psalm 31:15). When Daniel rebuked King Belshazzar for his pride and arrogance, he said, "But you did not honor the God who holds in his hand your life and all your ways" (Daniel 5:23). What was true for David and Belshazzar is just as true of us today. We have only to look around us to recognize it: Life is uncertain and unpredictable. "You do not know what a day may bring forth" (Proverbs 27:1).

Every breath we breathe is a gift from God. Most of the time we're not even aware of breathing; it's involuntary and unconscious. Yet both the air we breathe and the autonomic nervous system that regulates our breathing are God's gifts. Admittedly it's difficult to cultivate a sense of dependence on God for something we do unconsciously and automatically. But we can make it a point to pause periodically throughout the day to acknowledge our dependence on God just for life itself.

I take this moment to pause and acknowledge my total dependence on You, Almighty God. I acknowledge that I depend on You for "life and breath and everything else."

I acknowledge that I "do not know what a day may bring forth," and that therefore "my times are in your hands." I honor You as the One who holds in Your hand my life and all my ways. Acts 17:25; Proverbs 27:1; Psalm 31:15; Daniel 5:23

Yes, my every breath depends on You. In this regard our bodies are indeed like those of the animals—"when you take away their breath, they die and return to the dust." Psalm 104:29

So I worship You and praise You. "Let everything that has breath praise the LORD. Praise the LORD." Psalm 150:6

Before You, O God, I again acknowledge that by my own insight and reasoning I am utterly powerless to fully understand and accept Your truth; I depend on You even to understand the fact that I depend on You! I need Your enlightenment and teaching through the gift of Your Spirit, and for these I ask again: "Teach me your way, O LORD, and I will walk in your truth; give me an undivided heart, that I may fear your name." Psalm 86:11

FOR DAILY
SUSTENANCE

Paul told his Athenian audience (in Acts 17:25) that God gives not only life and breath but *everything else.* Through His providential rule over His creation, God sustains, feeds, and nourishes us. When Jesus taught us to pray, "Give us today our daily bread" (Matthew 6:11), He was teaching us to acknowledge our dependence upon our heavenly Father for the food we eat.

It's true that God has ordained our work as His usual way of supplying our food. As He said to Adam, "By the sweat of your brow you will eat your food" (Genesis 3:19). And even before Adam's sin and the consequent curse, God had "put him in the Garden of Eden to *work* it and take care of it" (Genesis 2:15). From the very beginning God ordained that we work for our food; yet at the same time Scripture says He gives it to us.

God gives us our food and other necessities of life by blessing our labors and making them productive. The

Scriptures consistently affirm this truth. For example, Psalm 104:14-15 states:

> *He makes grass grow for the cattle,*
> *   and plants for man to cultivate—*
> *   bringing forth food from the earth:*
> *wine that gladdens the heart of man,*
> *   oil to make his face shine,*
> *   and bread that sustains his heart.*

Some people believe that such passages mean only that God established the laws of nature and that these laws now operate quite apart from any divine intervention. Scripture, however, affirms God's direct and immediate control over nature. Consider the following passage:

> *He unleashes his lightning beneath the whole heaven*
> *   and sends it to the ends of the earth....*
> *He says to the snow, "Fall on the earth,"*
> *   and to the rain shower, "Be a mighty downpour."...*
> *The breath of God produces ice,*
> *   and the broad waters become frozen.*
> *He loads the clouds with moisture;*
> *   he scatters his lightning through them.*
> *At his direction they swirl around*
> *   over the face of the whole earth*

to do whatever he commands them.
He brings the clouds to punish men,
   or to water his earth and show his love.
      (Job 37:3,6,10-13)

It could be argued that the descriptions of God's actions in this passage are simply metaphorical expressions to denote the laws of nature. But note in the final verse God's twofold motive—to punish or to show His love (verse 13). Such discriminating motives cannot be ascribed simply to laws of nature that God has left to run their course.

God again confirms His direct control over our food and water supply in Amos 4:6-9:

"I gave you empty stomachs in every city
   and lack of bread in every town,
   yet you have not returned to me,"
      declares the LORD.
"I also withheld rain from you
   when the harvest was still three months away.
I sent rain on one town,
   but withheld it from another.
One field had rain;
   another had none and dried up.
People staggered from town to town for water
   but did not get enough to drink,

> *yet you have not returned to me,"*
>
> *declares the LORD.*
>
> *"Many times I struck your gardens and vineyards,*
>
> *I struck them with blight and mildew.*
>
> *Locusts devoured your fig and olive trees,*
>
> *yet you have not returned to me,"*
>
> *declares the LORD.*

Note God's direct, immediate control over the so-called acts of nature. "I gave you empty stomachs." "I also withheld rain from you." "I sent rain on one town, but withheld it from another." "I struck your gardens and vineyards." Nothing could be clearer than that the Jews were utterly dependent upon God for their food and water supply. When the Jews became rebellious and forgot this, God criticized them for what was missing in their thoughts: "They do not say to themselves, 'Let us fear the LORD our God, who gives autumn and spring rains in season, who assures us of the regular weeks of harvest'"(Jeremiah 5:24).

What was true for the Jews in the days of Amos and Jeremiah is just as true for us. Jesus reminded us that His Father "causes his sun to rise on the evil and the good, and sends rain on the righteous and the unrighteous" (Matthew 5:45).

Though the Amos passage speaks of God's judgment through the *withholding* of food and rain, the Bible just as clearly affirms His blessing through His gracious provision. Just before the Israelites entered Canaan, Moses warned them,

> *When you have eaten and are satisfied, praise the LORD your God for the good land he has given you.... Otherwise, when you eat and are satisfied, when you build fine houses and settle down, and when your herds and flocks grow large and your silver and gold increase and all you have is multiplied, then your heart will become proud and you will forget the LORD your God, who brought you out of Egypt, out of the land of slavery.... You may say to yourself, "My power and the strength of my hands have produced this wealth for me." But remember the LORD your God, for it is he who gives you the ability to produce wealth, and so confirms his covenant, which he swore to your forefathers, as it is today. (Deuteronomy 8:10,12-14,17-18)*

It is God who gives us the ability to work—and then, through His providential circumstances, blesses our work as He chooses.

Take time today (and at the beginning of each day) to acknowledge your dependence on God for life and breath and everything else, and to thank Him for specific blessings.

～

"Our Father in heaven, hallowed be your name.... Give us today our daily bread." Thank You for satisfying my physical hunger and thirst today.^{Matthew 6:9,11}

Thank You also for satisfying my spiritual hunger and thirst today. Lord Jesus, my Savior, I praise You as my true bread of life. Holy Spirit, my Counselor, I praise You as my true living water.^{John 6:35; 4:7,10-14}

"You are my God, and I will give you thanks." I will praise You and glorify You with thanksgiving.^{Psalms 118:28; 69:30}

"Praise the LORD, O my soul, and forget not all his benefits." ^{Psalm 103:2}

OUR DANGER

On the topic of our dependence upon God, all the scriptures we looked at earlier were of course addressed to people living in an agricultural economy where they could observe first-hand the work of God in providing or withholding their food. It's more difficult for us today when we buy our food in well-stocked supermarkets and when our refrigerators and pantry shelves have a week's supply or more of food.

In fact, with the comfortable living standard so many of us enjoy, we're in danger of having the same attitude Moses warned the Israelites about: "*My* power and the strength of *my* hands have produced this wealth for me" (Deuteronomy 8:17). If we substitute "my ability, education, and experience" for "my power and the strength of my hands," we can apply Moses' warning directly to our Christian culture today.

Complete dependence on God is a hard lesson to learn. We know we must work to provide the essentials of daily life, but in that very work we may easily forget that it is God who enables us to work; that it is God who gives us the intellectual and physical skills that qualify us to work and, yes, even provides the job itself. The God-fearing person recognizes this dependence on God and readily acknowledges Him as the source of all provision of the necessities and comforts of this life.

John Calvin addressed the importance of such acknowledgment in his *Institutes*. He wrote:

> *Until men recognize that they owe everything to God, that they are nourished by his fatherly care, that he is the Author of their every good, that they should seek nothing beyond him—they will never yield him willing service. Nay, unless they establish their complete happiness in him, they will never give themselves truly and sincerely to him.*[10]

In the same paragraph Calvin also spoke of "reverence joined with love of God." This was his description of fearing God. And he said this reverence and love for God are brought about by "the knowledge of his benefits." That is, a conscious awareness of our dependence on God as our Father who supplies our needs will increase our fear of Him—our reverential awe toward Him. It's equally true that the person who delights to follow God will seek to cultivate an ever-growing sense of dependence upon Him.

❧

To You, wise and loving God, I owe praise and thanksgiving for my ability to work. I choose today to remember this wonderful gift from Your hand and to acknowledge before You that my capacity for work is the result not of my own power and strength, but of **Your** power and strength.[Deuteronomy 8:10-18]

Almighty and Holy God, I acknowledge that I owe everything to You, that I am nourished by Your fatherly care, that You are the Author of my every good, and that I should seek nothing beyond Your will for me. You are my complete happiness, and I give myself truly and sincerely to You. "You are my Lord; apart from you I have no good thing."[Psalm 16:2]

I praise You because Your care of all things is constant and perfect. I give thanks to You, for You are good and Your faithful love and merciful kindness endure forever.[Psalm 136]

"Praise the LORD. How good it is to sing praises to our God, how pleasant and fitting to praise him!"[Psalm 147:1]

Depending on Him in Our Plans

Our dependence on God goes far beyond life and breath and the necessities of daily life. We're also dependent upon Him for the successful execution of our plans.

Few things are more common than planning. We plan to do the laundry today or go shopping tomorrow or take a vacation next month. Our calendars are full of things we plan to do. Turning to Scripture we find Paul planning to visit the believers at Rome on his way to Spain (Romans 15:24). Then we read in Proverbs that "The plans of the diligent lead to profit," and "Plans fail for lack of counsel" (21:5; 15:22).

Even God has plans. Job acknowledged to God that "no plan of yours can be thwarted" (Job 42:2), and Paul spoke of the "plan of him who works out everything in conformity with the purpose of his will" (Ephesians 1:11). So everyone makes plans, and planning is encouraged in the Bible.

Yet a certain type of planning is condemned in Scripture—planning that does not recognize our dependence on God for the successful execution of those plans.

James speaks to the issue this way:

*Now listen, you who say, "Today or tomorrow we will go to this or that city, spend a year there, carry on business and make money." Why, you do not even know what will happen tomorrow. What is your life? You are a mist that appears for a little while and then vanishes. Instead, you ought to say, "**If it is the Lord's will**, we will live and do this or that." (4:13-15)*

This passage addresses people making ordinary business plans. In a modern-day setting it is speaking to businesspeople who might plan to open a new store or introduce a new product line. It doesn't condemn such planning. It doesn't even condemn the plans to make money. What it does condemn are plans that don't take into account our dependence on God for their success.

Christians of my grandparents' generation often qualified their statements of intent with the phrase, "Lord willing." They were saying, "I plan to do such and such *if it is the Lord's will.*" In their writing they would end a sentence expressing some plan with the initials D.V., standing for the Latin phrase *Deo volente,* or "God willing." They were thereby acknowledging their dependence on God for the success of their plans.

Although the expression "Lord willing" undoubtedly became a meaningless cliché for many people, it's a practice well worth resuming because it forces us back to the realization of our absolute dependence on God. I'm not suggesting we overdo it—"I'm going to have cereal for breakfast, Lord willing." But we ought to use the phrase often enough to remind ourselves that we really are dependent on God for our plans, even for such mundane activities as having cereal for breakfast.

The events leading to my first wife's death (at least those events known to us) actually started on her birthday seventeen months earlier. Our son was home from college for the summer, and the three of us planned to go out to dinner that evening. My wife had what we thought was to be a routine doctor's appointment that morning. It was not routine. She was admitted immediately to the hospital without even the opportunity to go home and collect the personal things she would need for the hospital stay. Plans for an ordinary birthday dinner were squashed. I was again reminded that "Many are the plans in a man's heart, but it is the LORD's purpose that prevails" (Proverbs 19:21).

Someone has observed that our life is like a path having a thick curtain hung across it, a curtain that recedes before us as we advance, but only step by step. None of us can tell what is beyond that curtain. None of us knows what will happen to us tomorrow or even in the next hour. Often things go as planned, but sometimes our plans are thwarted.

Occasionally we hear that some public event has been canceled due to "circumstances beyond our control." The fact is, however, all circumstances are beyond our control. We are absolutely dependent upon God for the carrying out of our plans. The person who lives rightly before God not only acknowledges this but delights to do so. He or she finds great joy in realizing our dependence on the moment-by-moment care of our loving, sovereign heavenly Father.

I praise and thank You for the truth that "the plans of the LORD stand firm forever, the purposes of his heart through all generations." I worship You for the permanence and inevitability of Your plans, and I acknowledge that my own plans can never be anything remotely like that.[Psalm 33:11]

*And yet, because I sincerely long for my plans to be in agreement with Your will, I ask You today to open the eyes of my heart and fill me with the knowledge of Your will "through all spiritual wisdom and understanding." Let this be my mind-set and the desire of my heart as I make my plans; keep me sensitive to Your Holy Spirit's leading so that Your plans for me become **my** plans also. "Father in heaven, hallowed be your name, your kingdom come, your will be done on earth as it is* *in heaven." Your will be done in my life and in my plans, as it is in heaven. I want to be like the godly person Peter described, who "does not live the rest of his earthly life for evil human desires, but rather for the will of God."* Colossians 1:9; Matthew 6:9-10; 1 Peter 4:2

Once more, heavenly Father, I praise You for Your pure and perfect will. You are perfect and loving in all Your ways. Deuteronomy 32:4; Psalm 25:10

DEPENDING ON HIM
THROUGH OTHERS

One area of life where we're likely to realize our lack of independence and self-sufficiency is in our relationships with other people. All of us regularly encounter situations where we're dependent on the decisions or actions of someone else. These decisions or actions vary from the most routine and ordinary to ones affecting our future career or well-being.

I discovered I needed to see my doctor the day before I was to leave on a week's trip. I was totally dependent on the doctor's receptionist to work me into his schedule. It was her call. She easily could have said he had no more room in an already overcrowded day. I was dependent on her decision.

A Ph.D. candidate became a Christian in the midst of his doctoral studies. For that reason, a previously supportive but ungodly professor tried to block the granting of his degree. The student was seemingly at his mercy.

Between these two specific events—my very minor urgency and the graduate student's career-threatening crisis—

lies a vast number of situations in each of our lives where we depend on other people.

You may think I deal in trivial matters when I refer to such minor events as a doctor's appointment. One reason I do is because this is where we mostly live. Most of life is commonplace and ordinary. The Ph.D. candidate faced his degree crisis once. But a dozen times in his life he might need a doctor's appointment on short notice. He, along with each of us, needs to learn we're as dependent on God in the mundane events of life as we are in the extraordinary ones.

Furthermore, it's often easier to recognize our dependence on God in the major events than in the minor ones. A potentially life-changing crisis stands out in bold relief and immediately draws our attention to our dependence on Him. The more ordinary experiences tend to slip by without that recognition. Instead we are inclined to depend on ourselves and other people in these situations.

The person who fears and follows God, however, rejoices in the fact that we actually are *not* dependent on other people. We are dependent on God. The Bible consistently affirms that God is able to and does in fact carry out His plans through the decisions of people.

My favorite passage of Scripture on this subject is Proverbs 21:1: "The king's heart is in the hand of the LORD; he directs it like a watercourse wherever he pleases." If the heart of the most powerful monarch is in God's hand, then surely the decisions of doctors' receptionists and graduate-school professors are also subject to His control.

This truth does not nullify the freedom people have in their choices, nor does it reduce our responsibility to act prudently and discreetly when we are, humanly speaking, dependent on the decisions and actions of others. God works *through* people's wills, not against them, so that they freely make the choices He wants them to make. How God does this is of course a mystery. This is a part of God that He has not revealed to us. Nevertheless, it's a fact that God teaches us over and over in the Bible. (See, for example, Exodus 12:35-36; Ezra 1:1; Isaiah 45:13; Daniel 1:9; and 2 Corinthians 8:16-17.)

What is our responsibility to influence the decisions or actions of others? We can act presumptuously here in either of two opposite directions. One is to assume God is *not* in control, so that we rely totally on our efforts and our ability to influence others. The other extreme is to think that since God is in control, we need do nothing. But the wise course is to take all the steps we can take in a biblical manner and then to trust God for whatever the outcome may be. The extent of our reverential awe toward God will largely determine how well we're able to steer the proper course between the two extremes.

∾

Thank You, Father, that the hearts of everyone around me—
all those who influence and impact my life—are always truly
in Your hands, whether or not they love You or recognize Your
sovereignty. Proverbs 21:1

I trust in You and put my hope in You, not in people. O
God of hope, fill me with all joy and peace as I trust in You, so
that I might overflow with hope by the power of Your Holy
Spirit. "Guard my life, for I am devoted to you. You are my
God." Romans 15:13; Psalm 86:2

For myself and for all who are Your children, I praise You
that "in your unfailing love you will lead the people you have
redeemed." Exodus 15:13

I rejoice in Your perfect control of all circumstances,
including all the actions of others around me and every detail
of my life. "Many, O LORD my God, are the wonders you
have done. The things you planned for us no one can recount to
you; were I to speak and tell of them, they would be too many
to declare." Psalm 40:5

ACTIVE, ACTUAL RELIANCE

It isn't enough to passively believe we're dependent upon God for every aspect of our lives. We must *actively* rely on Him.

The primary way we do this is through prayer. J. I. Packer has written:

> *The prayer of a Christian is not an attempt to force God's hand, but a humble acknowledgment of helplessness and dependence. When we are on our knees, we know that it is not we who control the world; it is not in our power, therefore, to supply our needs by our own independent efforts; every good thing that we desire for ourselves and for others must be sought from God, and will come, if it comes at all, as a gift from His hands.*[11]

By praying we recognize our helplessness and dependence. By praying we recognize that we are not in control of our lives, our health, our plans, or the decisions other people make regarding us. We recognize, as Packer said, that we must seek God for every good thing we desire for ourselves and others.

As people who fear God and follow Him, we also recognize that God is not a divine bellhop, on call to respond to our every desire. We cannot use God simply to accomplish our aims. Rather we come expressing our need, committing it to Him, and leaving the outcome in His hands, because we know that He is our infinitely wise and loving heavenly Father.

At the same time, when we pray we should recognize God's power and His ability to do anything He chooses to do. When we study the prayers in the Bible, we notice how frequently God is addressed as the sovereign, all-powerful One who is able to answer those prayers. Asa, king of Judah, prayed:

> *LORD, **there is no one like you** to help the powerless against the mighty. Help us, O LORD our God, for **we rely on you,** and in your name we have come against this vast army. O LORD, **you are our God;** do not let man prevail against you. (2 Chronicles 14:11)*

Years later, Asa's son Jehoshaphat faced another military crisis. He prayed:

> *O LORD, God of our fathers, **are you not the God who is in heaven?** You rule over all the kingdoms of the nations. **Power and might are in your hand,** and no*

one can withstand you…O our God, will you not judge
them? For we have no power to face this vast army that is
*attacking us. We do not know what to do, but **our eyes are***
***upon you.** (2 Chronicles 20:6,12)*

Note how both Asa and Jehoshaphat acknowledged both
their helplessness and God's power.

We see this again in the prayers of the believers in the
infant church of Acts 4. When faced with the threats from
the Jewish Sanhedrin they prayed:

Sovereign Lord,…you made the heaven and the earth and
the sea, and everything in them. You spoke by the Holy
Spirit through the mouth of your servant, our father David:

> *"Why do the nations rage*
> *and the peoples plot in vain?*
> *The kings of the earth take their stand*
> *and the rulers gather together*
> *against the Lord*
> *and against his Anointed One."*

Indeed Herod and Pontius Pilate met together with the
Gentiles and the people of Israel in this city to conspire
against your holy servant Jesus, whom you anointed. They
did what your power and will had decided beforehand

should happen. Now, Lord, consider their threats and enable your servants to speak your word with great boldness. Stretch out your hand to heal and perform miraculous signs and wonders through the name of your holy servant Jesus. (Acts 4:24-30)

Consider how those early disciples acknowledged God's power and ability to answer their prayer. They addressed Him as "Sovereign Lord." They reminded God that the people responsible for the crucifixion of Jesus did "what your power and will had decided beforehand should happen"— they had simply been instruments to execute God's plan. Only when the disciples had acknowledged God's ability to answer their prayer did they make their request for personal boldness and for God's powerful working on their behalf.

Yes, it is true: "LORD, there is no one like you" to be my helper. So I ask You to help me, O Lord my God, for I rely on You. "O LORD, you are our God." 2 Chronicles 14:11

"O LORD, God of our fathers, are you not the God who is in heaven? You rule over all the kingdoms of the nations. Power and might are in your hand, and no one can withstand you." O my God, I have no power to face the daily challenges in my life; ultimately I don't really know what to do, except to keep my eyes upon You. 2 Chronicles 20:6,12

*You have commanded me to trust You with all my heart and to lean not on my own understanding. You have promised that "in quietness and trust" is my strength, and that You will keep me in perfect peace as I steadfastly trust in You. This is my desire, loving Father.*Proverbs 3:5; Isaiah 30:15; 26:3

"In you I trust, O my God." "I trust in you, O LORD; I say, 'You are my God.'" "I will say of the LORD, 'He is my refuge and my fortress, my God, in whom I trust.'" Psalms 25:2; 31:14; 91:2

*I love You, O Lord. "Teach me to do your will, for you are my God; may your good Spirit lead me on level ground." Do this, wise Father, for Your name's sake.*Psalm 143:10

*Loving Father, I worship You as the source of every single blessing in my life. "You are my Lord; apart from you I have no good thing." "All my fountains are in you." I have nothing that I did not receive from You.*Psalms 16:2; 87:7; 1 Corinthians 4:7

Beyond What We Can Anticipate

Admiring God's greatness is one of the major aspects of fearing God—of having a profound sense of reverential awe toward Him. This is not just passive admiration, however, such as the way we might admire a superb athlete in action. It is admiration at work—admiration that causes us to trust in God and in His power to answer our prayers.

Unfortunately our degree of trust in God often lies more in our ability to foresee a way in which He might answer our prayers than in our belief in His power. If we can't see *how* He can answer, we tend to doubt that He *will* answer. We pray, but if we were really honest with God and expressed our thoughts, this is how it would come out: "You know, Lord, that it's just a long shot. I don't see how You can possibly accomplish it, but I'm going to pray for it and see if something just might happen."

In 2 Kings 6 and 7, Israel's northern kingdom was besieged by the Aramean army. The food shortage became so critical that two women agreed to boil their children and eat them. When the king of Israel heard of this, in desperation he approached the prophet Elisha. Elisha announced that the siege would be lifted the next day and that food would be so plentiful that it would be on sale at bargain prices (2 Kings 7:1).

An officer who was with the king responded doubtfully, "Look, even if the LORD should open the floodgates of the heavens, could this happen?" (7:2). He didn't see how this could possibly occur, and therefore he didn't believe it.

To this Elisha responded, "You will see it with your own eyes,…but you will not eat any of it!" (7:2). He prophesied for the officer the humbling experience of seeing this blessing without being able to partake of it.

The next day four lepers sitting at the city gate reasoned with one another along these lines: "Let's go out to the enemy camp. If they kill us, we were only going to die anyway. On the other hand, they have food and they might give us some." When the lepers went out, they found the Aramean camp deserted; some supernatural noisemaking from God had caused the entire army to flee in fear, leaving behind their plentiful provisions.

After these four lepers had eaten and had stashed away a supply of treasure, they decided, "It isn't right for us to be out here enjoying all this alone. We ought to go back to the city and tell the good news." So they went back and told the people, who then rushed out to gather up the food. Just as

Elisha had prophesied, barley and wheat were on sale at bargain prices.

And what happened to the doubtful officer? The king ordered him to stand in the city gate and take charge of the operation. After the officer posted himself there, he was trampled to death by the masses of people going out for food. And so Elisha's entire prophecy was fulfilled.

Just after my thirtieth birthday, when I was still single, the Navigators asked me to take a three-year assignment overseas. One of the issues I had to work through was the fact that, as far as marriage prospects were concerned, I would be -out of circulation for those three years and would have to start from scratch once I returned. As events turned out, the day I arrived back in the States I had my first date with the young lady who would become my wife. We were married seven months later. There was no way I could have predicted how God would so arrange providential circumstances to bring that about.

As the account from 2 Kings and my own experience illustrate, God is not limited by our ability to see how He can answer our prayers or work on our behalf. Therefore we follow God and show true reverence for God by depending on Him even when we can't see how He might bring something to pass.

So our prayers should be both an acknowledgment of our own helplessness and dependence and an expression of our confidence that God can meet our needs in ways we could never anticipate. This is the way we actively rely on God and consciously depend on Him.

I mentioned earlier that a conscious dependence on God is not only for times of crisis but is to be sustained through all the events and activities of life. Obviously this practice has to be developed, since we are so accustomed to depending on ourselves most of the time. I also said the primary way we actively rely on God is through prayer. We can now see why the apostle Paul told us to "pray continually" (1 Thessalonians 5:17). *To depend on God continually is to pray continually.* We should seek to make it a practice to send up short, silent words of prayer throughout the day.

We should pray that we will display the fruit of the Spirit as we interact with other people throughout the day. We should pray for safety as we drive. We should pray for wisdom as we make decisions or do our work.

We should also send up prayers of thanksgiving during the day. We should be "always giving thanks to God the Father for everything, in the name of our Lord Jesus Christ" (Ephesians 5:20).

O God my Father, I acknowledge before You today my helplessness and dependence. I acknowledge as well my confidence that You can meet my needs in ways I could never anticipate. For Your pathways are "beyond tracing out!" Romans 11:33

It is true that we "cannot understand the work of God, the Maker of all things." You indeed perform "great things beyond our understanding." And though I can never truly comprehend Your ways, yet I know and believe that they are perfectly right. I praise and exalt and glorify You as the King of heaven, because everything You do is right and all Your ways are impartial and fair. Ecclesiastes 11:5; Job 37:5; Daniel 4:37

I truly admire Your greatness. "How great you are, O Sovereign LORD! There is no one like you, and there is no God but you." "Praise the LORD, O my soul. O LORD my God, you are very great." How awesome You are! How mighty and powerful You are! I glorify You as God and give thanks to You. You are worthy of all my praise forever. 2 Samuel 7:22; Psalm 104:1; Romans 1:21; 1 Chronicles 16:25

"How awesome is the LORD Most High, the great King over all the earth!" "Yours, O LORD, is the greatness and the power and the glory and the majesty and the splendor, for everything in heaven and earth is yours." Now, my God, I give You thanks and praise Your great name. Psalm 47:2; 1 Chronicles 29:11

Your "greatness no one can fathom." "I will proclaim the name of the LORD. Oh, praise the greatness of our God!" O Lord my God, how great Thou art! Psalm 145:3; Deuteronomy 32:3

Endless thanksgiving is truly and rightly due to You. I give thanks to You, O God my Father, "for everything, in the name of our Lord Jesus Christ." Ephesians 5:20

ACCEPTING EVERY CIRCUMSTANCE

If we truly acknowledge our dependence on God, we will also accept His providential workings in our lives, even those circumstances that are difficult for us and that we don't understand.

Earlier we saw in Psalm 139 how David practiced the conscious presence of God. We also see in this psalm how he trusted in God's sovereign providence in all of his life:

> *For you created my inmost being;*
> > *you knit me together in my mother's womb....*
> *All the days ordained for me*
> > *were written in your book*
> > *before one of them came to be. (verses 13,16)*

The Hebrew word for "inmost being" is literally "kidneys," a word used in Hebrew idiom for the center of emotions and moral sensitivity. David was essentially saying, "You created my personality." David ascribed to God not only the creation of his physical body but also the makeup of his personality or temperament. David was not aware of the genetic code we know about today. But he was writing under the inspiration of the Holy Spirit who designed the genetic code in the first place. Without being aware of how all this takes place, David was telling us how thoroughly God superintends the genetic code and the biological process. God is fully and directly involved in fashioning each of us into the person that He wants us to be—in both physical traits and temperament.

I don't know how many generations back we have to go to determine our genetic makeup, but however far it is, God was overseeing the entire process. We are who we are (apart from sin, of course) because God made us that way.

Not only did God create us the way we are, He also ordained life's path for us. Look again at verse 16: "All the days ordained for me were written in your book before one of them came to be." All the experiences of David's life were written down in God's book before he was even born. This refers not simply to God's prior knowledge of our lives but to His unique plan for each of us. It includes the family into which we were born, the opportunities we have throughout life, and all our successes as well as our failures and disappointments. It includes the circumstances we welcome and those we would just as soon avoid. All the events of our lives were written in God's book before we were born.

God is causing all these events—both what we call "good" and what we call "bad"—to work together for our good, that is, to make us more and more like Christ. That's why we're told to "give thanks in all circumstances, for this is God's will for you in Christ Jesus" (1 Thessalonians 5:18). Note that this instruction immediately follows Paul's exhortation to "pray continually" (verse 17). We should then cultivate the practice of praying continually and always giving thanks, and doing both in all circumstances because we know that even those difficult trials we shrink from are designed for our ultimate good.

This expression of conscious dependence on God is both a characteristic of profound reverence for God and a means of growing in that reverence. As we follow God, we will come to recognize more each day that not only is He the Creator of our world and all that is in it, but He is also its faithful sustainer and the sovereign ruler of all events. And in that knowledge we will bow in awe before Him.

In my circumstances today, I give You thanks even for obstacles and frustrations, for disappointments and trials. I trust in You,

and my heart's deepest desire is to fully trust in You no matter how painfully difficult my circumstances might become.
1 Thessalonians 5:18; Job 13:15

Thank You that even when the circumstances of my life cause me grief, I can still be assured that You personally designed those very circumstances to prove the genuineness of my faith, and that this will result finally in "praise, glory and honor when Jesus Christ is revealed." 1 Peter 1:7

I rejoice in Your perfect will for my life, now and forever, as You lead me day by day. "You have made known to me the path of life." "You broaden the path beneath me, so that my ankles do not turn." Psalms 16:11; 18:36

And this is my prayer as I accept every circumstance You bring me as I follow You on the path of life: "Teach me your way, O LORD; lead me in a straight path." Psalm 27:11

SPIRITUAL DEPENDENCE

In exploring our dependence on God, our focus has been in the temporal areas of life—the daily provision of our needs, the successful execution of our plans, the decisions and actions of other people that affect us, the providential circumstances that come our way, and even life itself. One obvious major area we haven't touched on is the spiritual dimension of life.

I have reserved this topic until now, not because it's the least important or even the most important, but because this is the dimension of our lives where we're most apt to recognize our dependence on God.

Most of us are quite familiar with Jesus' words, "Apart from me you can do nothing" (John 15:5). We readily acknowledge the truth of Jesus' statement, though we apply it imperfectly. We do pray, however, over the Sunday school lessons we teach, the evangelism opportunities we have, the messages we prepare, and most other activities that are clearly "spiritual" in our eyes. Even in this realm, though, the more trained and experienced we become in these so-called spiritual activities, the more we're tempted to rely on our training and experience rather than on God.

I was meeting with a man in a one-to-one discipling relationship. One day he said he would like to discuss a particular topic the next week. I thought to myself, "I'm so familiar with that topic I could discuss it now without any preparation." So I didn't prepare. Worse, I didn't pray about it. I was depending completely on my knowledge and experience. As I was driving to our appointment, it dawned on me how totally dependent on myself I was that day. I repented of my self-sufficient attitude and acknowledged to God that only He could make our time fruitful.

Have you ever done anything similar? Each of us should examine ourselves to see how much of our spiritual dependence is really in ourselves rather than in God.

In actuality, there really should be no sharp distinction for us between the spiritual and the temporal. All of life should be spiritual in the sense that all of life should be lived in the fear of God and to the glory of God.

Conscious dependence on God is a spiritual habit that must be developed. Take time to consider how you might grow more in this area of your life. Here are some suggestions:

- Think ahead through your day. Acknowledge your dependence on God for all your foreseen activities of the day, asking for His direction and enablement in each of them.

- Commit to Him also the *unforeseen* events of the day, again asking for His ability to respond to each in a way pleasing to Him.
- Seek to develop the habit of continually offering throughout the day those short, silent prayers that recognize your powerlessness and His power. Use whatever reminder strategies will help you develop this habit, such as sticky notes in strategic places or the hourly chime on your wristwatch alarm. Don't consider such methods too childish or "unspiritual" to help you learn this important habit.
- Most of all, pray regularly that God will help you and make you more and more aware that you are in fact dependent on Him for life and breath and everything else.

Finally, don't be discouraged by failure. We have all been too much shaped by our culture of independence, so developing this attitude of dependence on God does take time. It's worth the effort though, because as you follow God and grow in your conscious dependence on Him, you'll increasingly experience joy.

Great and wise and holy and loving God, I come before You again to acknowledge my dependence on You in everything this day.

I praise You as my faithful Shepherd and my Guide. "For great is your love, higher than the heavens; your faithfulness reaches to the skies." In this moment I enter Your gates with thanksgiving and Your courts with praise, and give thanks to You and praise Your name, for You are good and Your love endures forever, Your faithfulness through all generations.
Psalms 108:4; 100:4-5

*In all my ministry, let what I say be **Your** words, and let whatever I do be done with the strength You alone provide, so that in all things You may be praised "through Jesus Christ. To him be the glory and the power for ever and ever. Amen."*
1 Peter 4:11

Need of Jesus

LORD JESUS,

I am blind, be thou my light,

> *ignorant, be thou my wisdom,*

> *self-willed, be thou my mind.*

Open my ear to grasp quickly thy Spirit's voice,

> *and delightfully run after his beckoning hand;*

Melt my conscience that no hardness remain,

> *make it alive to evil's slightest touch;*

When Satan approaches may I flee to thy wounds,

> *and there cease to tremble at all alarms.*

Be my good shepherd to lead me into the green pastures of
> *thy Word,*

> *and cause me to lie down beside the rivers of its comforts.*

Fill me with peace, that no disquieting worldly gales

> *may ruffle the calm surface of my soul.*

Thy cross was upraised to be my refuge,

Thy blood streamed forth to wash me clean,

Thy death occurred to give me a surety,

Thy name is my property to save me,

By thee all heaven is poured into my heart,

> *but it is too narrow to comprehend thy love.*

I was a stranger, an outcast, a slave, a rebel,

> *but thy cross has brought me near,*

> > *has softened my heart,*

has made me thy Father's child,

has admitted me to thy family,

has made me joint-heir with thyself.

O that I may love thee as thou lovest me,

that I may walk worthy of thee, my Lord,

that I may reflect the image of heaven's first-born.

May I always see thy beauty with the clear eye of faith,

and feel the power of thy Spirit in my heart,

for unless he move mightily in me

no inward fire will be kindled.

—THE VALLEY OF VISION

Part III

I Will Follow You, O God...

LIVING ALL OF LIFE
UNDER YOUR AUTHORITY

For the LORD your God is God of gods and Lord of lords,

the great God, mighty and awesome.

<small>DEUTERONOMY 10:17</small>

Give thanks to the God of gods.

His love endures forever.

Give thanks to the Lord of lords.

His love endures forever.

<small>PSALM 136:2-3</small>

On his robe and on his thigh he has this name written:

KING OF KINGS AND LORD OF LORDS.

<small>REVELATION 19:16</small>

HE IS LORD

We live in a day of bumper-sticker slogans. Some are amusing and elicit a chuckle from us; others are repugnant and disgusting. Some are downright dangerous, such as "Question Authority." Of course all of us have trouble with authority at times. But questioning authority—even resisting it—seems to have been elevated to a national virtue. It is spreading like a virus throughout our society.

The fact is, however, that God has built authority into the entire fabric of our moral universe. Society, even on a purely human plane, could not function without it. The opposite is anarchy: a state of lawlessness or disorder due to a lack of authority.

God established His authority over mankind with Adam in the Garden of Eden: "And the LORD God commanded the man, 'You are free to eat from any tree in the garden; but you must not eat from the tree of the knowledge of good and evil, for when you eat of it you will surely die'" (Genesis 2:16-17). The effect of this single prohibition was to confront Adam head-on with God's absolute authority and thus to face him with the demand for clear-cut obedience. Of course, Adam and Eve did not obey, and authority has been a problem for us ever since, both in resisting it and abusing it. We must therefore learn what it means both to submit to authority and to exercise it properly in all our various relationships to authority structures.

Foremost among the fundamental traits of those who follow God is the commitment to live all of life under God's authority. It should go without saying that those who fear God and follow Him submit to His authority gladly and willingly. We see God insisting on His authority (in its most basic meaning of "the right to command") from Genesis to Revelation. The Ten Commandments (Exodus 20:1-17) are an expression of God's authority. Moses spoke of God's "commands, decrees and laws" that the Israelites were to obey (Deuteronomy 6:1). The psalmist said, "You have laid down precepts that are *to be fully obeyed*" (Psalm 119:4). God's people are clearly reminded of this in Jeremiah 7:22-23: "For when I brought your forefathers out of Egypt and spoke to them…I gave them this command: *Obey me,* and I will be your God and you will be my people. Walk in all the ways I command you, that it may go well with you." Jesus said, "If you love me, you will *obey* what I command" (John 14:15; see also verses 21 and 23). All these references assume divine authority to issue commands and to call everyone to account for obedience to them at the final judgment (Revelation 20:12).

Clearly the issue of God's authority over His creatures is one of the most basic principles of Scripture. It underlies everything else. We know that the Bible, overall, is the revelation of God's plan of redemption for sinners through Jesus Christ. But that plan of redemption is basically the re-establishment of His authority over rebellious human beings whom He calls out of darkness into the kingdom of His Son (Acts 26:18; Colossians 1:13). The whole purpose of Jesus' death was to "redeem us from all wickedness [that is, from rebellion against His authority] and to purify for himself a people that are his very own, eager to do what is good [to live under His authority]" (Titus 2:14).

Bringing people everywhere under the authority of Jesus Christ is the essence of His Great Commission to the church. Jesus said, "All authority in heaven and on earth has been given to me. Therefore go and make disciples of all nations" (Matthew 28:18-19). I first learned this passage from the King James Version, which reads "all power" instead of "all authority." Since *power* connotes ability, I originally understood Jesus' statement to be what I called the "enabling clause"—that He was saying, "Since I have all power, you will be successful in carrying out My commission."

Authority, however, speaks primarily of the right to

command, although it carries with it the idea of the corresponding power to enforce that command. *To make disciples, then, is to bring people under the sway of Christ's authority.* It is to teach them to obey everything He has commanded us.

Baptist commentator John Broadus wrote this about Jesus' words:

> To disciple a person to Christ is to bring him into the relation of pupil to teacher, "taking his yoke" of **authoritative** instruction, accepting what he says as true because he says it, and submitting to his requirements as right because he makes them.... We see then that Christ's intimated **authority** is not only the basis of our duty to disciple others, but the basis of all true discipleship.[12] (emphasis added)

Everything Jesus teaches us to do is, of course, wise and good, and the more we grow in the Christian life the more we see this to be true. But we obey Him not because we judge His commands to be wise and good, but because He is God and has a perfect right to be believed and obeyed. We do not, to use a popular expression, "make Christ Lord of our lives." He *is* Lord. Our duty is to acknowledge His Lordship and submit to His authority.

Ask yourself this question: Do I wholeheartedly acknowledge God's authority, both in His precepts and His providences, in my life? Do I resent or question any of His providential circumstances in my life?

*Before You, O God, I acknowledge again that by my own insight and reasoning I'm utterly powerless to accept or even understand Your truth. I depend totally on **Your** enlightenment and teaching through the gift of Your Spirit, and for these I ask again: "Teach me your way, O LORD, and I will walk in your truth; give me an undivided heart, that I may fear your name."* Psalm 86:11

*In my heart and mind, let me be still and know that You are God. In this quiet moment, I worship You. In quiet reverence I acknowledge Your total sovereignty and authority over my life. "You are **my** God, and I will give you thanks; you are **my** God, and I will exalt you."* Psalms 46:10; 118:28

It is You who made me, and I am Yours, the sheep of Your pasture. "You are God…I am your servant." "You alone, O Lord, are God." "You, whose name is the Lord…you alone are the Most High over all the earth." Psalm 100:3; 1 Kings 18:36; 2 Kings 19:19; Psalm 83:18

Jesus, my Lord and my God, I praise You. You are God! "Truly you are the Son of God!" Your "name is the Word of God." You are "the image of the invisible God." You are "the Holy One of God," "the Righteous One," "the Living One." You are *"the Alpha and the Omega…who is, and who was, and who is to come, the Almighty."* ^{Matthew 14:33; Revelation 19:13; Colossians} 1:15; John 6:69; Acts 22:14; Revelation 1:18; 1:8

You are the Lord of lords and King of kings, and Your kingdom will never end. "Your throne, O God, will last for ever and ever, and righteousness will be the scepter of your kingdom." Revelation 17:14; Luke 1:33; Hebrews 1:8

And You are "the Lamb of God, who takes away the sin of the world!" "To the Lamb be praise and honor and glory and power, for ever and ever!" John 1:29; Revelation 5:13

Amen.

THE AUTHORITY
OF SCRIPTURE

To live under Christ's authority necessarily means to live under the authority of His Word. I read a sermon in which the speaker said that we're to live in obedience to Jesus Christ, not to Scripture. This, however, is drawing a false and unwarranted distinction between Christ and His Word.

How can I obey anyone in authority over me if I do not have that person's instructions or commands? In the matter of authority we cannot separate a person from his or her words. Christ has spoken to us through the Bible. The only way I can live in obedience to Him is to live in obedience to His Word as given to us in Scripture.

It is not "bibliolatry" to place the authority of Scripture on a par with the authority of Christ. It is true that all authority rests in the *person* of Christ, but it is equally true that He expresses His authority through His written Word. To separate the authority of Christ from the authority of His

Word, as some seek to do, is a subtle ploy to undermine the authority of Scripture.

And when we speak of Jesus' words, we mean *all* Scripture, not just His spoken words recorded in the four Gospels, Acts, and Revelation. "All Scripture is God-breathed" (2 Timothy 3:16). As Peter explained it, "Men spoke from God as they were carried along by the Holy Spirit" (2 Peter 1:21). In the realm of spiritual authority, Scripture's words from Paul or James or Peter are as authoritative as those from Jesus, because it was the Spirit of Jesus who inspired those men, leading them to say exactly what He wanted.

We must do more, however, than agree that all Scripture is authoritative for our lives. To follow God, we must submit to it as our rule of faith and duty, believing what it says and doing what it commands. As John Bunyan said, "It is not the knowledge of the will of God, but our sincere complying therewith, that proves we fear the Lord."[13]

This compliance with His will includes letting the Bible mold our opinions and values. It is common today to hear someone in a Sunday school class or Bible study discussion group saying, "I think such and such," simply giving his or her opinion on an issue. No appeal is made to Scripture. Instead we must constantly ask ourselves, "What does the Bible say on this issue?"

Some years ago, when I was working in the business and financial affairs of the Navigators, my boss called me into his office to discuss a major problem. Another staff member had verbally committed the organization to accept a piece of real estate in return for a lifetime income to the donor (a common practice among nonprofit organizations). My boss had gone to look over the property and discovered to his dismay that the property, an old estate, was in a sad state of repair and fraught with problems. He concluded it would be unwise to accept the property; yet a verbal commitment had been made.

He called me in to discuss what we should do. Since no contract had been signed, he was trying to determine if we could back out of the deal with integrity. "Can you think of any scripture that will give us guidance?" he asked. I suggested Psalm 15, which says, "LORD, who may dwell in your sanctuary? Who may live on your holy hill?... [He] who keeps his oath even when it hurts" (verses 1 and 4). My boss said, "That's our answer." He concluded we must keep our verbal commitment.

That's an example of what it means to live under the Bible's authority. We could have sat for hours and discussed our opinions on what to do. Most likely we would have been seeking justification for backing out of the deal. And we probably would have found one if we had avoided the Bible and sought the answer in our own opinions.

Not every decision we face has a Scripture passage speaking so directly to it as Psalm 15 spoke to our real-estate deal.

We might be surprised, however, to find how clearly God's Word addresses our issues if we're familiar enough with Scripture to find the appropriate passages. When no specific passage comes to mind, we should always ask, "What *principles* in the Bible give guidance in this instance?"

Paul used this method when discussing the right of Christian workers to be supported by those who benefit from their ministry:

> *Who serves as a soldier at his own expense? Who plants a vineyard and does not eat of its grapes? Who tends a flock and does not drink of the milk? Do I say this merely from a human point of view? Doesn't the Law say the same thing? For it is written in the Law of Moses: "Do not muzzle an ox while it is treading out the grain." Is it about oxen that God is concerned? Surely he says this for us, doesn't he? Yes, this was written for us, because when the plowman plows and the thresher threshes, they ought to do so in the hope of sharing in the harvest. (1 Corinthians 9:7-10)*

Paul appealed to a command in the Old Testament that had nothing to do with the subject at hand. He looked beneath the Old Testament application to a specific farming situation and found the underlying principle. He then applied the principle to a contemporary situation and found scriptural guidance. Note that he appealed to the *authority* of

Scripture to establish the right of Christian workers to be supported in the ministry. Too often today we spend hours in a committee meeting discussing an issue without once asking ourselves, "What does the Bible say on this subject?"

Life cannot be compartmentalized into spiritual and secular but must all be lived as God directs us in His Word. This means consistently and habitually reading and studying the Bible to determine what we should believe and how we should live. The God-fearing person seeks after "the knowledge of the truth that leads to godliness" (Titus 1:1). He or she wants to know the truth, not just intellectually but in a way that promotes growth in godliness.

Ask yourself this question: Do I seek to live all of life under the authority of God's Word, believing what it says and seeking to apply its teachings to *every* area of my life?

Your Word is not only my authority but my delight! "I delight in your commands because I love them." "Your statutes are my delight; they are my counselors." And so I pray, "Direct me in the path of your commands, for there I find delight."
Psalm 119:47,24,35

Loving Father, thank You for the light You give me in the Bible through Your Holy Spirit. "Your word is a lamp to my feet and a light for my path." Your commands "are radiant, giving light to the eyes." Because You are holy, Your words "are flawless, like silver refined in a furnace of clay, purified seven times." Psalms 36:9; 119:105; 19:8; 12:6

I praise You, Lord God, that "you have laid down precepts that are to be fully obeyed." Your doing this was entirely fitting and proper, for "I know, O LORD, that your laws are righteous." "All your commands are trustworthy." "Righteous are you, O LORD, and your laws are right." Psalm 119:4,75,86,137

"You are good, and what you do is good." I praise You for the perfect goodness of Your Word, and for Your graciousness in giving it to us. Psalm 119:68

True Father, I praise You for the clean and complete truth of Your Word. "All your words are true." "Your word is truth."
Psalm 119:160; John 17:17

Eternal Father, I praise You as well for how everything You have said will continue forever, "living and active." "Your word, O LORD, is eternal; it stands firm in the heavens." "Your statutes are forever right." "You established [your statutes] to last forever." Hebrews 4:12; Psalm 119:89,144,152

I praise You for how Your Word is so amazingly rich and profound. "To all perfection I see a limit; but your commands are boundless." "Your statutes are wonderful." Psalm 119:96,129

"How sweet are your words to my taste, sweeter than honey to my mouth!" Thank You for the sweet and precious gift of Your Word! "May my lips overflow with praise, for you teach me your decrees. May my tongue sing of your word."
Psalm 119:103,171-72

HUMAN AUTHORITY

Living under God's authority also means we willingly live under the human authority structures He has established. We're to live under the authority of those whom God has placed over us in government, in the church, in the family, and in the workplace.

Here we immediately encounter sensitive issues. It seems to be one thing to acknowledge God's authority but quite something else to submit to human authority structures, especially when we have a choice. The "Question Authority" bumper sticker may express it quite blatantly, but to some degree that attitude lurks in every one of our hearts as one expression of our fallen sinful nature.

To guide us in our thoughts on this topic, I want to make three general observations about human authority. First, the Bible clearly teaches that certain human authority relationships have been established by God. To resent these relationships is to resent God's authority.

Second, human authority is not a status or privilege to be exploited for personal goals, but a responsibility to be borne for the benefit of others.

Third, your place in an authority structure (whether exercising authority or submitting to it) does not determine your personal significance. This is especially true among Christians, who "are all one in Christ Jesus" (Galatians 3:28).

There has never been a time in my life when I wasn't subject to some authority, even beyond that of government. Until I was an adult, I was subject to my parents and to various teachers and coaches. As an officer in the navy, I was under authority and I exercised authority. The same was true during my brief stint in secular employment. It has been true for more than forty years' service with the Navigators. During all these years, despite a few difficult experiences, I simply accepted the fact that this is the way God ordained life. I've never felt submission to authority made me less of a person.

In the days to come, as we explore these human authority structures—in government, in the church, in the family, and in the workplace—take time to pray over each of these authority relationships. Is any one of them troublesome to you? Ask yourself this question: Am I chafing—either openly or secretly in my heart—under any God-ordained human authorities? Are there any relationships here in which I need to change my attitude or actions?

Don't answer with a simple yes or no. Be specific about situations that may be troublesome to you, either as one under authority or as the one exercising authority. What steps do you need to take to establish God-fearing, biblical relationships in those situations? Don't just say, "I need to be more submissive to my husband," or "I need to be more loving to my wife." Where exactly do you need to be more submissive or more loving? Only by dealing with particulars will we make progress in following God.

As you consider God's authority and the authority structures He has established, keep in mind that He exercises His authority in love. As I was writing this, my mind was drawn to Galatians 2:20 where Paul wrote of "the Son of God, who loved me and gave himself for me." It is the Son of God who loves *me* and gave Himself for *me* who now claims all authority over me. How can I resist the authority that springs from such a heart of love?

◦◦

"You are good, and what you do is good." I praise You for Your perfect goodness and graciousness in giving us human authority structures during the time of our life on earth.[Psalm 119:68]

Sovereign Lord, I pray, "Your kingdom come, your will be done" in my life as it is in heaven.[Matthew 6:10]

Thank You, Lord God, that Your authority over me is never separated from Your love for me. I thank You "that you, O God, are strong, and that you, O Lord, are loving."[Psalm 62:11-12]

Thank You, Lord Jesus, for Your heart of love from which You claim all authority over me. For You loved me and gave Yourself for me.[Galatians 2:20]

GOVERNMENTAL AUTHORITY

The classic Scripture passage regarding governmental authority is Romans 13:1-7. Notice especially the purposes for which God established this authority:

> *Everyone must submit himself to the governing authorities, for there is no authority except that which God has established. The authorities that exist have been established by God. Consequently, he who rebels against the authority is rebelling against what God has instituted, and those who do so will bring judgment on themselves. For rulers hold no terror for those who do right, but for those who do wrong. Do you want to be free from fear of the one in authority? Then do what is right and he will commend you. For he is God's servant to do you good. But if you do wrong, be afraid, for he does not bear the sword for nothing. He is God's servant, an agent of wrath to bring punishment on the wrongdoer. Therefore, it is necessary to submit to the*

authorities, not only because of possible punishment but also because of conscience.

This is also why you pay taxes, for the authorities are God's servants, who give their full time to governing. Give everyone what you owe him: If you owe taxes, pay taxes; if revenue, then revenue; if respect, then respect; if honor, then honor.[14]

Governmental authority has been established by God for our good. This is true in the most primitive societies with their tribal chiefs as well as in the complex cultures of large nations. Moreover, God in His providence has established the *particular* governmental authority under which we live. Paul no doubt had in mind both the general concept and the specific application of the Roman government. Paul was never theoretical; he was always thinking of concrete situations. So he was telling Roman believers to submit to the Roman authorities under which they lived.

Note also that governmental authority is part of God's plan for society. Paul even referred to those in authority as "God's servant[s]." They are His agents to execute punishment on those who do wrong. This speaks to the most elemental function of government—the preservation of law and order for the public good.

In our time, government has become more complex. We have speed limits, zoning regulations, food and drug laws, environmental laws, and on and on. We often consider them excessive or unfair. I spent twenty-five years overseeing the Navigators' compliance with all those laws, regulations, and ordinances, so I understand why we bristle at them. Remember, however, that though Roman law was not as extensive as ours, it was also excessive and unfair at times. Nevertheless, Paul said we must submit, because government has been instituted by God.

This word *submit* goes deeper in its meaning than simple adherence to specific laws or ordinances. It indicates recognition of our subordinate state in the whole realm of governmental authority and consequently our willing subservience to that authority. If we rebel against it, we are rebelling against what God has instituted.

Of course our situation is noticeably different from Paul's day. Under our representative form of government, it's at least theoretically possible for us to address issues through the legislative or judicial processes. Apart from such lawful means of change, however, our responsibility is to submit to the authority of government.

There are two ways we can rebel: in our actions and in our attitudes. The word *submit* speaks to both. You and I don't usually rebel in our actions because of possible consequences. What we have to watch more often is a rebellious attitude.

The one exception to our submission is when authorities

clearly seek to stop our obedience to God. At that point our response should be, to use Peter's words, "We must obey God rather than men!" (Acts 5:29; see also 4:19-20).

We must be careful, however, in applying that scriptural principle. In our city, a church of about a hundred people was meeting in a private home, creating parking problems in the neighborhood. The pastor bitterly resisted the city's efforts to enforce its zoning laws, claiming abridgment of the church's religious freedom. In my opinion this was not the case. God in His Word had not told the church to meet at that house. Instead it seems the church was disobeying God by resisting the city's legitimate authority to establish zoning regulations. We can easily become confused in applying the principle of obeying God rather than man.

If the government forbids believers to meet together at all, that's a different issue. This of course is happening in many countries today, and we support believers' efforts there to obey God rather than human authority.

*"You are good, and what you do is good." I praise You for Your perfect graciousness in establishing governmental authority for our good.*Psalm 119:68

I praise You, Lord, as the Sovereign God over all the nations. I worship You as the Judge of all the earth. You are coming to judge the world in righteousness and the peoples in truth. And although as history progresses, the nations in their pride and prosperity continue to "rage like the raging sea" and to "roar like the roaring of great waters," yet the day is coming when they will finally be still and know that You are God; You will be exalted among the nations, You will be exalted in the earth. Psalm 96:13; Isaiah 17:12; Psalm 46:10

In Your Word, I read Your promises: "I will show my greatness and my holiness, and I will make myself known in the sight of many nations." "My name will be great among the nations, from the rising to the setting of the sun." You have promised a coming day when "men will look to their Maker and turn their eyes to the Holy One of Israel." You have promised, "The LORD will lay bare his holy arm in the sight of all the nations." Ezekiel 38:23; Malachi 1:11; Isaiah 17:7; 52:10

Thank You for exalting Your Son, Jesus, to the highest place and giving Him the name that is above every name, that at His name every knee will bow in heaven and on earth and under the earth, and every tongue confess that He is Lord. Philippians 2:9-11

"Hallelujah! For our Lord God Almighty reigns. Let us rejoice and be glad and give him glory!" Revelation 19:6-7

AUTHORITY
IN THE CHURCH

I was shocked the first time I heard a message from Hebrews 13:17: "Obey your leaders and submit to their authority. They keep watch over you as men who must give an account. Obey them so that their work will be a joy, not a burden, for that would be of no advantage to you." It had never occurred to me that I should submit to those in leadership in our church. I had to do a lot of hard thinking on that message before I came to the conclusion that I had the wrong attitude toward spiritual authority.

Leadership in the church is serious business. God holds church leaders accountable for the spiritual welfare of their people. They are to watch over us "as men who must give an account."

Paul said to the Ephesian elders, "Keep watch over yourselves and all the flock of which the Holy Spirit has made you overseers. Be shepherds of the church of God, which he bought with his own blood" (Acts 20:28). Paul pointed out that it was the Holy Spirit who made these men elders. We may vote on our elders and deacons or the calling of a pastor, but we should do so in utter submission of our minds and hearts to the Holy Spirit's guidance. He is the One to appoint overseers, and He is the One to whom they're accountable. Our responsibility is to submit to their leadership. We're also commanded to "respect" them and to "hold them in the highest regard in love because of their work" (1 Thessalonians 5:12-13).

Balancing our responsibility to submit to church leaders is their responsibility to govern in a biblical manner. They must first remember that they're responsible to God and will one day have to give an account to Him for their leadership. Then they're to serve as examples to those entrusted to their care, exercising their authority without being authoritarian (1 Peter 5:3).

I appeal to you to honestly assess your attitude toward those in leadership over you in the church. Is it one of submission or independence?

"You are good, and what you do is good." I praise You for Your perfect goodness and graciousness in giving us leaders in our church. Thank You for these shepherds of Your church and for their hard work on our behalf. Psalm 119:68; Acts 20:28; 1 Thessalonians 5:13

I acknowledge before You that their authority derives from You, O God of wisdom. Thank You for Your reminder in Scripture that in the church we ultimately "have only one Master" and we "are all brothers." "For us there is but one God, the Father, from whom all things came and for whom we live; and there is but one Lord, Jesus Christ, through whom all things came and through whom we live." I praise and thank You for the precious gift of our unity, for "there is one body and one Spirit…one Lord, one faith, one baptism; one God and Father of all, who is over all and through all and in all." Matthew 23:8; 1 Corinthians 8:6; Ephesians 4:4-6

HUSBANDS AND WIVES

A third authority structure God established is the family. The classic passage for authority relationships in the family is Ephesians 5:22–6:9, where Paul deals with three family relationships—husband and wife, parents and children, and masters and slaves.

We're confronted at once in this passage with one of the most sensitive and controversial issues among Christians today: What did Paul teach about the submission of wives to husbands? Consider the relevant verses carefully:

> *Wives, submit to your husbands as to the Lord. For the husband is the head of the wife as Christ is the head of the church, his body, of which he is the Savior. Now as the church submits to Christ, so also wives should submit to their husbands in everything.*
>
> *Husbands, love your wives, just as Christ loved the church and gave himself up for her to make her holy, cleansing her by the washing with water through the word, and to present her to himself as a radiant church, without stain or*

wrinkle or any other blemish, but holy and blameless. In
this same way, husbands ought to love their wives as their
own bodies. He who loves his wife loves himself. (5:22-28)

The basic issue boils down to this: Does a believing wife
have an obligation before God to submit to the headship
authority of her husband, or did Paul teach a mutual submission of husband and wife to each other? The advocates of
the latter view cite Ephesians 5:21, "Submit to one another
out of reverence for Christ," in support of their position.

Much has been written on this subject from both points
of view, and I don't expect to say anything new here. Let me
mention also that this is a subject on which godly, sincere
Christians disagree. Whichever side we take, we need to be
gracious and loving toward those with whom we disagree.

Let's look first at the passage exhorting us to mutual submission (Ephesians 5:21). On this I've found the words of
New Testament scholar F. F. Bruce to be helpful. He points
out this verse's place in introducing a "household code" that
represents "a special application of the Christian grace of
submission." Bruce writes,

> *Christians should not be self-assertive, each insisting on get-*
> *ting his or her own way. As the Philippian believers are told,*
> *they should be humble enough to count others better than*
> *themselves and put the interests of others before their own,*

following the example of Christ, who "emptied himself,"
"humbled himself," and "became obedient," even when the
path of obedience led to death on the cross.... Even those
who fill positions of responsibility and honor in the Chris-
tian community, to whom their fellow-believers are urged to
render submission and loving respect, earn such recognition
by being servants, not lords.

Bruce then examines the verses that follow the mutual
submission command:

While the household code is introduced by a plea for
mutual submissiveness, the submissiveness enjoined in the
code itself is not mutual. As in the parallel code in Colos-
sians 3:18-4:1, wives are directed to be subject to their hus-
bands, children to be obedient to their parents, and slaves
to their masters, but the submissiveness is not reciprocated:
Husbands are told to love their wives, parents to bring
up their children wisely, and masters to treat their slaves
considerately.[15]

When we read in Ephesians 5:24 that wives should submit to their husbands *as the church submits to Christ*, it
seems clear that Paul didn't intend a mutual submission relationship between husbands and wives, since a mutual sub-

missiveness between Christ and the church is unthinkable. Similarly, no one would interpret the mutual submission principle to mean parents and children should be mutually submissive to each other. Therefore, I conclude that Paul meant for wives to submit to their husbands, just as a simple reading of the text would lead us to think he means, however unpalatable it may seem to some.

But the passage doesn't indicate an absolute surrender of the wife's will. It doesn't say she exists merely to serve her husband. Nor does it forbid her from partnering with her husband in managing the home and family. It *does* teach that she should cultivate a willingness to yield to her husband's authority and to follow his leadership. Above all it means she should not try to compete with him as the head of the home.

Does this submission mean the wife is inferior to the husband or that she's a second-class citizen in the marriage? Not at all, since believers are all one in Christ (Galatians 3:28). The fact that I'm to submit to a person in governmental authority does not make me inferior to that individual. It's simply a recognition of his God-ordained role in an authority structure God has established. The same should be true in the home.

That this is Paul's teaching seems to be clear from his repetition of this principle in Colossians 3:18, "Wives, submit to your husbands, as is fitting in the Lord," and in Titus 2:3-5,

"Older women…can train the younger women…to be subject to their husbands." The same principle is taught in 1 Peter 3:1-7, applying even to wives with unbelieving husbands.

As for the husband, he is not to exercise his leadership in an authoritarian or self-serving manner, requiring blind and absolute submission to his will or insisting that he always be served. Rather he's to love his wife as Christ loved the church and gave Himself up for her (Ephesians 5:25). This obviously denotes a sacrificial, self-giving love that seeks to promote the spiritual, emotional, and physical well-being of his wife. It means the husband should be considerate and thoughtful about the needs of his wife and any impositions he might make upon her.

Perhaps the best insight on the attitude a husband should have toward his authority role comes from the words Jesus spoke to His disciples: "You know that the rulers of the Gentiles lord it over them, and their high officials exercise authority over them. Not so with you. Instead, whoever wants to become great among you must be your servant, and whoever wants to be first must be your slave—just as the Son of Man did not come to be served, but to serve, and to give his life as a ransom for many" (Matthew 20:25-28). This is how the mutual submission principle (Ephesians 5:21) is worked out in daily life.

∽

"You are good, and what you do is good." I praise You for Your perfect goodness and graciousness in giving us an authority structure for our families. Psalm 119:68

Thank You for the holy and beautiful gift in every marriage of husband to wife and wife to husband. Thank You for the holy gift of the marriage covenant. Genesis 2:24; Malachi 2:14-16

I praise You, Lord Jesus, for Your example to all husbands in how You loved the church, Your bride, and gave Yourself up for her to make her holy. Ephesians 5:25-26

PARENTS AND CHILDREN

As for parental authority, Paul's teaching that children should obey their parents (Ephesians 6:1-3) is straightforward enough. I want to point out, however, that we parents have a duty to train our children to obey. Our responsibility in our God-given role as parents is to see that our children submit to our authority. It's especially important that a father teach his children to submit to their mother's authority as much as to his. Teaching our children to respect and obey those in authority over them—beginning with Mom and Dad—is one of the ways we help them learn to fear the Lord (Deuteronomy 6:1-2). The lack of this teaching is one of the most serious problems in Christian families today.

Not only must we learn to fear God by keeping His commandments; we must also teach our children to do likewise. We must not only teach them to obey; *we must teach them to obey in the fear of the Lord.* Ours is the same purpose Moses set forth in Deuteronomy 6:2: "so that you, your *children* and their children after them may fear the LORD your God as long as you live by keeping all his decrees and commands that I give you, and so that you may enjoy long life."

I fear we aren't following through on the teaching pattern Moses gave us in verses 6 and 7:

These commandments that I give you today are to be upon your hearts. Impress them on your children. Talk about them when you sit at home and when you walk along the road, when you lie down and when you get up.

God holds us as parents responsible for teaching our children to obey Him. We cannot pass this off to Sunday school teachers or the Christian school. Those agencies may supplement our efforts, but the primary responsibility lies with us.

Even the instruction given in Christian homes is too often mere moralism. Parents want their children to be good, to stay out of trouble, to not get drunk or use drugs. Little effort is made to teach them to fear God and obey Him out of reverence for Him. Because of this, many young people do not see themselves as sinners desperately in need of a Savior. Many of them go through the motions of "accepting Christ" without ever being convicted of their personal need of Him. I realize conviction of sin is the work of the Holy Spirit, but He does use human agencies, and His primary design is to use parents.

Our children need to be taught what it means to fear God, to love Him and obey Him. They need to be taught the primacy of loving their neighbor as themselves and how this is worked out in treating others as they want to be treated. They need to understand that obedience is possible only through the enabling power of the Holy Spirit. Above all, they need to see that their only hope of acceptance by a holy God, both in this life and eternity, is through faith in the shed blood and righteous life of our Lord Jesus Christ.

That God holds parents responsible for teaching their children is a truth that predates the Mosaic Law. Concerning Abraham, God said, "For I have chosen him, so that he will direct his children and his household after him to keep the way of the LORD by doing what is right and just, so that the LORD will bring about for Abraham what he has promised him" (Genesis 18:19). May we who are parents accept our responsibility, as Abraham did, to teach our children to fear the Lord by obeying Him. Only then are we ourselves obeying God.

In Ephesians we see that Paul, as was his custom, once again turned from addressing those under authority to those exercising it—in this case, from children to fathers. His instruction is, "Do not exasperate your children" (Ephesians 6:4; see also Colossians 3:21). This is another warning against authoritarianism. The father's authority should be exercised for the spiritual and moral benefit of all the children. That's essentially the meaning of Paul's next words: "Instead, bring them up in the training and instruction of the Lord" (Ephesians 6:4).

❧

Our loving Father in heaven, hallowed be Your name. I praise You as the source of all fatherhood and parenthood, the One from whom Your entire family in heaven and on earth is named. Matthew 6:9; Ephesians 3:15

I praise You that "every good and perfect gift is from above"—from You!—"coming down from the Father of the heavenly lights." Thank You for the good and perfect gift of my family. James 1:17

Almighty God, thank You for Your perfect example as a Father to Your only begotten Son, Jesus Christ, whom You loved before the creation of the world. In Your love for Him You "placed everything in his hands." When He came to earth, You gave Him Your name, and You lovingly showed Him everything You were doing. You listened to Him and talked with Him. You taught Him what to say and how to say it. You glorified Him, and even now You continue to glorify Him. John 3:35; 5:20; 8:54; 11:41; 13:31-32; 12:28,49-50; 17:1,5,11,24

Thank You also for Your perfect example as a Father to me and to all Your redeemed children. "How great is the love the Father has lavished on us, that we should be called children of God! And that is what we are!" Yes, how lavishly vast is Your fatherly love! Therefore through Your Holy Spirit within me I lovingly call You "Abba, Father." 1 John 3:1; Romans 8:15; Galatians 4:6

I worship and praise You as my "Father of compassion and the God of all comfort." "Your compassion is great, O Lord." And I worship and praise You as "the glorious Father." 2 Corinthians 1:3; Psalm 119:156; Ephesians 1:17

Thank You, Lord Jesus, for Your perfect example as a Son to Your Father. You honored Him and glorified Him. Obediently and faithfully, You learned from Him what to do and what to say, and You glorified Him by completing the work He called You to do and showed You how to do. You perfectly reflected Your Father's character and actions. You always loved Him and did exactly what He commanded You to do. When the terrible hour came for Your sacrifice and Your separation from Your Father, You obeyed His will and drank the bitter cup He had ordained for You. And even now You continue to bring Him glory. John 5:17,19-23,26,36; 8:28,49; 12:28; 14:10-11,13,24,31; 17:4; 18:11

"To our God and Father be glory for ever and ever. **Amen.** *"* Philippians 4:20

AUTHORITY
IN THE WORKPLACE

The New Testament principles underlying the master-slave relationship apply in today's employer-employee situations. The classic passage addressing this is Colossians 3:22-25. Notice how submission to a God-ordained authority structure is a concrete expression of our fear of the Lord.

> *Slaves, obey your earthly masters in everything; and do it, not only when their eye is on you and to win their favor, but with sincerity of heart and reverence for the Lord. Whatever you do, work at it with all your heart, as working for the Lord, not for men, since you know that you will receive an inheritance from the Lord as a reward. It is the Lord Christ you are serving. Anyone who does wrong will be repaid for his wrong, and there is no favoritism.*

If we substitute employees for slaves and employers (owners, managers, supervisors) for masters, the passage is

straightforward enough. We're to work at our jobs or profes-
sions as working for the Lord. God is our ultimate employer,
and we're to serve Him with reverence ("fearing the Lord,"
verse 22, NASB).

Paul's instruction to masters (and to whoever has authority in the workplace) is to provide those under their authority "with what is right and fair, because you know that
you also have a Master in heaven" (Colossians 4:1). The
employer's authority is not absolute. He also is under the
authority of God Himself, and God will hold him accountable for how he treats his employees. In the Old Testament,
God's people were warned not to treat hired workers ruth-
lessly, but instead to "fear your God" (Leviticus 25:43). This
should be the attitude of Christian employers today—treating employees fairly out of the fear of the Lord.

Our problem is not in understanding these principles
but in applying them. When I was a young officer in the
navy, I served on a small ship under a commanding officer
who was very difficult to work with. The man had almost
no people skills, and none of the officers (including me)
respected him. Then one day in the course of Bible study, I
encountered 1 Timothy 6:1: "All who are under the yoke of
slavery should consider their masters worthy of full respect,
so that God's name and our teaching may not be slandered."

I wasn't exactly under a yoke of slavery, though sometimes I felt I was. In any event the principle of respecting one

in authority over me was impressed upon me by the Holy Spirit applying His Word to my heart. I was convicted of my sinful attitude and immediately began taking steps to correct it. I said nothing to our captain or to the other officers, none of whom were Christians. Yet somehow the captain sensed something had changed in our relationship. Months later I was transferred from that ship. As I was about to leave, the captain called me into his stateroom and said, "Bridges, I really hate to see you go."

It isn't easy to submit to the authority of those who do not exercise it in a sensitive manner. But our submission should not hinge on their manner, as slaves are told in 1 Peter 2:18-19: "Submit yourselves to your masters with all respect, not only to those who are good and considerate, but also to those who are harsh. For it is commendable if a man bears up under the pain of unjust suffering because he is conscious of God." Note that last phrase. "Because he is conscious of God" probably means "because he is aware of God's all-seeing eye and desires to please Him." This is consistent with Paul's instructions for slaves to obey their masters out of the fear of the Lord.

❧

In consciousness of You, O God, I acknowledge Your all-seeing eye. I know that You see everything I do, and that You are the final Inspector for all my work.

I also acknowledge before You my genuine desire to please You, because of the gift of Your Holy Spirit within me.

In this consciousness of You and with confidence in You, I praise You and thank You. "The LORD is my strength and my shield; my heart trusts in him, and I am helped. My heart leaps for joy and I will give thanks to him." Psalm 28:7

Father, this is my prayer: "May the favor of the Lord our God rest upon us; establish the work of our hands for us—yes, establish the work of our hands." Psalm 90:17

And I praise and thank You that the day is coming when everyone will recognize You as the only Sovereign Authority— "The LORD will be king over the whole earth. On that day there will be one LORD, and his name the only name." Zechariah 14:9

The Divine Will

O LORD,

I hang on thee; I see, believe, live,

> *when thy will, not mine, is done;*

I can plead nothing in myself

> *in regard of any worthiness and grace,*
>
> *in regard of thy providence and promises,*
>
> *but only thy good pleasure.*

If thy mercy make me poor and vile, blessed be thou!

Prayers arising from my needs are preparations for future
> *mercies;*

Help me to honour thee by believing before I feel,

> *for great is the sin if I make feeling a cause of faith.*

Show me what sins hide thee from me

> *and eclipse thy love;*

Help me to humble myself for past evils,

> *to be resolved to walk with more care,*

For if I do not walk holily before thee,

> *how can I be assured of my salvation?*

It is the meek and humble who are shown thy covenant,

> *know thy will, are pardoned and healed,*
>
> *who by faith depend and rest upon grace,*

who are sanctified and quickened,
who evidence thy love.
Help me to pray in faith and so find thy will,
by leaning hard on thy rich free mercy,
by believing thou wilt give what thou hast promised;
Strengthen me to pray with the conviction
that whatever I receive is thy gift,
so that I may pray until prayer be granted;
Teach me to believe that all degrees of mercy arise
from several degrees of prayer,
that when faith is begun it is imperfect and must grow,
as chapped ground opens wider and wider until rain
comes.

So shall I wait thy will, pray for it to be done,
and by thy grace become fully obedient.

—THE VALLEY OF VISION

Part IV

I Will Follow You, O God...

DELIGHTING IN GENUINE OBEDIENCE

I press on to take hold of that for which Christ Jesus took hold of me....
Forgetting what is behind and straining toward what is ahead,
I press on toward the goal to win the prize
for which God has called me heavenward in Christ Jesus.

PHILIPPIANS 3:12-14

The LORD is my strength and my song;
he has become my salvation.
He is my God, and I will praise him,
my father's God, and I will exalt him.

EXODUS 15:2

Let your compassion come to me that I may live,
for your law is my delight.

PSALM 119:77

EXPRESSING OUR LOVE FOR GOD

Just as there is a close connection in Scripture between the fear of God and obedience (as we discussed in this book's introduction), so also the Bible draws a close connection between love to God and obedience. For example, 1 John 5:3 reads, "This is love for God: to obey his commands." And Jesus said, "Whoever has my commands and obeys them, he is the one who loves me" (John 14:21). This connection is also brought out frequently in the Old Testament. One of many instances is Deuteronomy 6:5: "Love the LORD your God with all your heart and with all your soul and with all your strength." This verse occurs in the middle of a longer section having to do with obedience to God. Words such as *commands, decrees,* and *laws* fill the passage (verses 1-9). Israel is to "be careful to obey" (verse 3). The commands were to be constantly on the hearts and minds of the people (verses 6-9). It's in this context of obedience that God's people are instructed to love Him with all their hearts. To love God, then, is to obey Him.

The people of Israel related to God on the basis of His covenant with them. In ancient Middle Eastern cultures the word *love* is used in treaties, or covenants, to denote the faithful adherence to the directives of the overlord. Meredith Kline, who has extensively studied ancient Near Eastern covenants, writes, "When swearing allegiance to the suzerain [a superior feudal lord or overlord] the vassals at times declared: 'Our lord we will love.' And a vassal wishing to clear himself of suspicion of infidelity protests that he is the king's great servant and 'friend' (literally, one who loves the suzerain)." Then Kline points out that "to love the suzerain meant precisely to serve him by obeying the particular demands stipulated in his treaty."[16] Israel was to love God, then, by obeying the commands and decrees of His covenantal law given to them at Mount Sinai.

Since we find a direct connection between fearing God and obedience to Him, plus a direct connection between loving God and obedience to Him, we can conclude that fearing God and loving God are also closely connected. Deuteronomy 10:12-13 draws all these attitudes and actions together in a single sentence:

> *And now, O Israel, what does the LORD your God ask of you but to fear the LORD your God, to walk in all his ways, to love him, to serve the LORD your God with all your heart and with all your soul, and to observe the LORD's commands and decrees that I am giving you today for your own good?*

The words *walk, serve,* and *observe* are three different
ways of expressing the same thought: Obey God. Israel was
to fear God, love God, and obey Him. The commandments,
then, provided a framework within which the Israelites
could express both their reverence for God and their love of
Him. The same is true for us today. Our obedience to God's
moral will found throughout Scripture is an expression of
our love for God and our reverence of Him.

We saw earlier that the fear of God expresses itself fun-
damentally in submission to the authority of God and His
Word. Without meaning to detract from that concept, we
can also acknowledge that submission to authority, even in
its most positive sense, may often be cold and impersonal.
We can submit to someone in authority over us without
either liking or loving the person, or even getting to know
the person. We submit because it's the appropriate thing to
do. We must go further than that with God, however.

Yes, we must acknowledge His authority in its most
basic sense—His right to command. God's instructions
in Scripture are not merely guidelines or advice for better
living. They are *commands* that are to be *fully* obeyed
(Psalm 119:4). Furthermore, apart from faith in Christ and
His atoning work, all who fail to obey the entire law are
under a curse (Galatians 3:10). So we must not in any way
temper or water down submission to God's authority as an
expression of our fear of Him. But we should submit out of

love and reverence for Him. That is, we should obey Him with our whole heart.

And our submission should not be with a slavish fear, but with a fear of reverential awe. There is a tension between the way we should view God in His transcendent majesty and the way we behold Him as our Father. Both sides of this tension work together to produce the right motive and the effective motivation to obey God.

Ask yourself this question: Do I obey God only out of a sense of duty or because I love Him and fear Him?

I worship You, holy and awesome God. I trust in You; I praise You, and I give thanks to You. I love You because You first loved me. "I love you, O LORD, my strength." 1 John 4:19; Psalm 18:1

I praise You for Your personal request of me to love You with all my heart and with all my soul and with all my mind and with all my strength. How honored I am that You so greatly desire my love…and so much of it! Mark 12:30

Before You, O God, I acknowledge once more that by my own insight and reasoning I am utterly powerless to accept or even understand how to love You and obey You and follow You. I depend totally on Your enlightenment and teaching through the gift of Your Spirit, and for these I ask once more: "Teach me your way, O LORD, and I will walk in your truth; give me an undivided heart, that I may fear your name." Psalm 86:11

OBEDIENCE
IN RELATIONSHIPS

To fear God by obeying Him means that we seek to follow all of His commands for us. We must not pick and choose or seek to reinterpret only some of them. We may willingly obey such commandments as "You shall not murder," "You shall not commit adultery," "You shall not steal." But are we as quick to obey "You shall not covet…anything that belongs to your neighbor" (Exodus 20:13-15,17)? Similarly, do we truly believe Jesus' words that anger fits under the prohibition against murder and lust in the category of adultery (Matthew 5:21-22,27-28)?

Too often we define sin in terms of those actions that may be least troublesome to us—drunkenness, dishonesty, sexual immorality, abortion, homosexuality. We see the sinfulness of society around us but not the sin in our own hearts—critical and judgmental attitudes (which are actually evidences of pride), selfishness, gossip, backbiting, insisting on our own way, and seeking to manipulate or intimidate others.

The one place where Paul warned us not to grieve the Holy Spirit is not in scriptures dealing with dishonesty or immorality, but in a section dealing with our speech and other interpersonal relationships (Ephesians 4:29-32). He said, for example, "Do not let any unwholesome talk come out of your mouths, but only what is helpful for building others up according to their needs, that it may benefit those who listen" (4:29).

Unwholesome speech includes not only vulgar language (which Paul addressed in Ephesians 5:4), but any kind of speech that tends to tear down the persons addressed or those spoken about—complaints, gossip, slander, critical words, harsh and impatient words. This prohibition is absolute: "Do not let *any* unwholesome talk come out of your mouths, but *only* what is helpful for building others up." Immediately after this Paul said, "And do not grieve the Holy Spirit." We grieve the Holy Spirit not only with dishonesty or immorality but also by our gossip, complaints, and sharp words.

If we express our fear of God by keeping *all* His decrees and commands as Moses said (Deuteronomy 6:2), then we must give attention to our interpersonal relationships. Consider, for example, the following list from Romans 12:

- Love sincerely (verse 9).
- Be devoted to one another in brotherly love (verse 10).
- Honor others above yourself (verse 10).

- Share with others in need (verse 13).
- Practice hospitality (verse 13).
- Bless those who persecute you (verse 14).
- Rejoice with those who rejoice (verse 15).
- Mourn with those who mourn (verse 15).
- Live in harmony with one another (verse 16).
- Do not be proud or conceited (verse 16).
- Do not repay evil for evil (verse 17).
- Seek to live at peace with everyone (verse 18).
- Do not seek revenge (verse 19).
- Overcome evil with good (verse 21).

These instructions may sound like a laundry list of moralisms, something we might hear at a service club luncheon. We agree with them. We give lip service to them. But do we honestly seek to practice them?

These words are not just moralisms from the pen of the apostle Paul; they are the words of God. If we accept the authority of Scripture, then we must view every one of these relational actions as God's commands to be carried out in the fear of God. We honor one another above ourselves *in the fear of the Lord.* We practice hospitality *in the fear of the Lord.* We overcome evil with good *in the fear of the Lord.*

Ask yourself these questions: Do I define sin primarily in terms of the gross sins of society, or do I first recognize my own personal sins of pride, selfishness, judgmental attitudes, gossip, discontent, and so on? And as I review the list of interpersonal relationship actions from Romans 12:9-21, what is my greatest need from among them at this time?

O God, because You first loved me, my deep and genuine desire is to love other people as You do, and with Your love. I praise and thank You for giving me this desire and for giving me Your own example of love.[1 John 4:19; John 13:15,34]

I say to You once more, "I love you, O LORD, my strength."[Psalm 18:1]

Because I love You, I pray this prayer: "Teach me to do your will, for you are my God; may your good Spirit lead me on level ground." Do this, wise Father, "for your name's sake." Teach me to love as I am loved.[Psalm 143:10,11]

THE GREAT COMMANDMENT AT GREAT COST

The flagrant sins in society around us are serious, and what is more distressing, they are creeping into our churches. But in our focus on other people's sins we tend to forget that Jesus said the first commandment is to "love the Lord your God with all your heart and with all your soul and with all your mind.... And the second is like it: 'Love your neighbor as yourself'" (Matthew 22:37,39). All the Law and the Prophets hang on those two commandments (verse 40).

Notice how Paul picked up on this priority of love in two of his letters:

> *The commandments, "Do not commit adultery," "Do not murder," "Do not steal," "Do not covet," and whatever other commandment there may be, are summed up in this one rule: "Love your neighbor as yourself." Love does no*

harm to its neighbor. Therefore love is the fulfillment of the
law. (Romans 13:9-10)

You, my brothers, were called to be free. But do not use your
freedom to indulge the sinful nature; rather, serve one another
in love. The entire law is summed up in a single command:
"Love your neighbor as yourself." (Galatians 5:13-14)

In both instances Paul said that the command "Love your neighbor as yourself" sums up the Law, a similar statement to that which Jesus made. Likewise James referred to the commandment "Love your neighbor as yourself" as the "royal law" (James 2:8).

I fear we do not take these words seriously enough. We don't embrace the fact that our first and highest duty in the Christian life (apart from loving God) is to love one another. We focus on "manageable sins" that we seldom commit and neglect the greatest commandment, though God brings it before us again and again in His Word. The command to love one another appears in some form in all but four books of the New Testament. (And even in those four it is present indirectly; see Acts 4:32-35; 20:35; 3 John 6; Jude 21-23; and Revelation 2:19).

Some fifty passages in the New Testament command us to love one another. Consider the comprehensiveness and intensity of this command in the following verses:

"And live a life of love, just as Christ loved us and gave himself up for us as a fragrant offering and sacrifice to God." (Ephesians 5:2)

"And over all these virtues put on love, which binds them all together in perfect unity." (Colossians 3:14)

"The goal of this command is love, which comes from a pure heart and a good conscience and a sincere faith." (1 Timothy 1:5)

"Keep on loving each other as brothers." (Hebrews 13:1)

"Above all, love each other deeply, because love covers over a multitude of sins." (1 Peter 4:8)

How can we miss it? How can we seem to focus on everything else but love?

I think the answer is that love is costly. To forgive in love costs us our sense of justice. To serve in love costs us time. To share in love costs us money. Every act of love costs us in some way, just as it cost God to love us. But we are to live a life of love just as Christ loved us and gave Himself for us at great cost to Himself.

∽

Holy God, I acknowledge that my first and highest duty in the Christian life (apart from loving You) is to love my brothers and sisters in Christ.

Through the indwelling presence of Christ within me, I ask You to make me "rooted and established in love." Give me power "to grasp how wide and long and high and deep is the love of Christ, and to know this love that surpasses knowledge." Let me "live a life of love," just as Christ loved me and gave Himself up for me as a fragrant offering and sacrifice to You.
Ephesians 3:17-19; 5:1-2

O God, I praise You for the great cost of Your salvation for me. You did not spare Your own Son, but delivered Him up for me. Romans 8:32

Lord Jesus Christ, I praise You for the great cost of Your love for me. While I was still a sinner, You died for me. Romans 5:8

"To you, O Lord, I lift up my soul. You are forgiving and good, O Lord, abounding in love to all who call to you." "To your name be the glory, because of your love and faithfulness."
Psalms 86:4-5; 115:1

"I will sing of the LORD's great love forever; with my mouth I will make your faithfulness known through all generations." Psalm 89:1

Never Less than the Golden Rule

How can we get a handle on such an immense subject as love? What does it mean, for example, to love your neighbor as yourself?

In that familiar verse known as the Golden Rule, Jesus said, "So in everything, do to others what you would have them do to you, for this sums up the Law and the Prophets" (Matthew 7:12). To treat others as we would like to be treated "sums up the Law and the Prophets." This is exactly what Paul said about loving your neighbor as yourself in Romans 13:9. Therefore to love your neighbor as yourself means to treat your neighbor as you would like to be treated. Love may sometimes mean more than that, but it certainly never means less.

Of course your neighbor isn't just the person next door. It is your spouse, your children, your parents, your in-laws, your roommate, coworkers, fellow church members, and even other drivers on the freeway. Your neighbor is any-one you come in contact with and interact with in some way.

To treat these neighbors as you would like to be treated sounds simple enough, but it has wide-ranging implications. If you don't like to be gossiped about, you shouldn't gossip about others. If you like others to be patient and forbearing with you, be patient and forbearing with others. If a husband wouldn't want his wife to admire other men in a sexual way, he shouldn't look that way at other women.

Consider love's description in 1 Corinthians 13:4-5: "Love is patient, love is kind. It does not envy, it does not boast, it is not proud. It is not rude, it is not self-seeking, it is not easily angered, it keeps no record of wrongs." Doesn't every one of these expressions describe the way you want other people to treat you? Then this is the way you must treat others if you want to be obedient to God. Obedience is more than not committing adultery; it is being patient with your spouse. Obedience is more than not murdering someone; it is not being easily angered with him or keeping a record of his wrongs against you.

The statement "Love your neighbor as yourself" is only the last half of a sentence in its original occurrence in Scrip-ture. The full sentence reads, "Do not seek revenge or bear a grudge against one of your people, but love your neighbor as yourself. I am the LORD" (Leviticus 19:18). Note that it's in the context of bearing a grudge or seeking revenge that we're told to love our neighbor as ourselves. *This means love always forgives.* "Since God so loved us, we also ought to love one another" (1 John 4:11). God loved us and forgave us at great cost to Himself, the cost of His own dear Son. We in turn are to love others, even at great cost to ourselves. Sometimes the cost is tangible—for example, in damage to our reputation if we've been slandered. At other times the cost may be a willingness to not see justice done as a condition of forgiveness.

So we both fear God and love Him by obeying His law. And we obey His law by loving others, by treating them as we want to be treated. Living the Christian life is difficult but not complicated. Yes, at times we may agonize over the right course of action. But if we seriously seek to follow this royal law, "Love your neighbor as yourself" (James 2:8), we'll usually know what to do.

Ask yourself this question: Is there some person in day-to-day contact with me whom I am not treating as I would like to be treated?

Thank You, mighty God, for loving me into Your salvation. "I will be glad and rejoice in your love." Psalm 31:7

I give thanks to You, gracious Father, for You are good; Your faithful love and Your merciful kindness endure forever.
Psalm 136:1

Now, O Lord, "continue your love to those who know you." In my life today, deal with me according to Your great love. "Remember, O Lord, your great mercy and love, for they are from of old." Psalms 36:10; 25:6

Each day, "let the morning bring me word of your unfailing love, for I have put my trust in you. Show me the way I should go, for to you I lift up my soul." This is my prayer for each day, for myself and for those I love: "Satisfy us in the morning with your unfailing love, that we may sing for joy and be glad all our days." Psalms 143:8; 90:14

Loving Lord, I praise You for being patient and kind. I thank You that Your love "does not delight in evil but rejoices with the truth." I praise You that Your love "always protects, always trusts, always hopes, always perseveres," and that Your love never ends. 1 Corinthians 13:4-8

Give me more of this love—Your love—in my love for others, I pray.

To You, O God my Father and the Father of our Lord Jesus Christ, "be the glory and the power for ever and ever. Amen." 1 Peter 4:11

FULLY RESPONSIBLE, FULLY DEPENDENT

But once we know what to do in order to love others and thereby obey God's law, we may not want to do it. The cost seems too high. We might have to humble ourselves, inconvenience ourselves, forgo our sense of justice. So we may evade those issues by rationalizing.

There are other times, many in fact, when we want to obey but can't seem to do it. We identify with Paul when he said, "I have the desire to do what is good, but I cannot carry it out. For what I do is not the good I want to do; no, the evil I do not want to do—this I keep on doing" (Romans 7:18-19).

Through all these instances we learn that we're unable to live the Christian life in our own moral strength and willpower. We learn the truth of Jesus' statement, "Apart from me you can do nothing" (John 15:5). But God also intends that we learn the converse truth: "I can do everything through him who gives me strength" (Philippians 4:13). God wants us to learn both the necessity and the positive results of depending upon the Holy Spirit to enable us to live the Christian life.

One of the most fundamental truths we must learn in Christian growth is that we are responsible, yet dependent. That is, we are responsible to obey God's commands. We are responsible for our sin. We cannot blame the devil or other people. We sin because we choose to sin. We do not obey because we choose not to obey. Yet at the same time we do not have the resources within ourselves to obey. We are completely dependent upon the Holy Spirit.

Notice how this principle is taught by Paul in Philippians 2:12-13:

> *Therefore, my dear friends, as you have always obeyed— not only in my presence, but now much more in my absence—continue to work out your salvation with fear and trembling, for it is God who works in you to will and to act according to his good purpose.*

First, Paul urged them to apply themselves diligently to working out their salvation, displaying daily the evidence of their new life through obedience to God's commands. And of course what Paul wrote to the Philippian believers is applicable to us today; we, too, are responsible to work out our salvation.

This is no secondary endeavor to be attended to after we've fulfilled all our other responsibilities. Rather it should be our highest priority. As Jesus said, we're to seek *first* His kingdom and His righteousness. Our salvation is to be worked out in how we carry out our daily activities. This is no easy task to be accomplished on the backstroke. According to New Testament commentator William Hendriksen, the meaning and tense of the verb "work out" indicate "continuous, sustained, strenuous effort."[17]

But Paul's exhortation does not suggest that we have the ability to do this by our own power. Rather the Philippians were told to work out their salvation *with fear and trembling*— "conscious of their own insignificance and weakness and sinfulness and fallibility," as New Testament Professor Jan J. Müller writes, "and full of trembling and holy fear before God whose will is to be done, and for whose honour they have to work, and to whom an account will have to be given."[18]

It is an awesome thought to realize the extent of our responsibility before God and yet to be painfully aware that we do not have within ourselves the ability to carry out the least of His commandments. That's why Paul hastened to add those encouraging words of verse 13: "for it is God who works in you to will and to act according to his good purpose."

Obedience to God is very much our responsibility, but it is a responsibility that must be carried out in utter dependence on the Holy Spirit. We work as He enables us to work. We cannot make one inch of progress in obeying God apart from His working in us to enable us.

To work hard, but only in dependence on the Holy Spirit, is a difficult lesson to learn. We know we must work hard, but in that very work we can easily slip into reliance on our own willpower instead of depending on the Holy Spirit to work in and through our wills. Yet this dependence on the Holy Spirit is absolutely essential to fearing God by obeying Him.

∽

Loving Lord, I have tasted and seen that You are good. I worship You. I take refuge in You, and I stay close to You. Psalm 34:8

Because of Your Word, I know that I can do nothing apart from You. I also know that with You—in Your strength—"I can do everything." John 15:5; Philippians 4:13

Thank You that You are working in me to will and to act according to Your good purpose. Because of this wonderful truth, teach me how to work out my salvation with fear and trembling. Continue Your good and perfect work in my life! I acknowledge that I am responsible before You, in every moment of my life, to obey Your will. I also acknowledge that I cannot carry out this responsibility except in utter dependence on Your Holy Spirit. I can "work out" my salvation only as You enable me to. Philippians 2:12-13

Therefore, all the glory for my life will be Yours alone. For from You and through You and to You are all things. To You "be the glory forever! Amen." Romans 11:36

Day 30

ALWAYS UNDER THE GOSPEL

We need to also keep in mind that our obedience is never the means of earning any merit or blessing from God. Though we're to make every effort to obey, our best works always fall short of that perfection God's law demands. We never obey God with *all* our heart and soul and mind, and we never perfectly love our neighbor as ourselves. Rather, "whoever keeps the whole law and yet stumbles at just one point is guilty of breaking all of it" (James 2:10).

This is why we must learn to live *under the gospel* every day. The gospel is not just for unbelievers; it is for believers also, because we are still sinners. Every day we need the reassurance that all our sins are forgiven (Colossians 2:13) because Christ paid for them all on the cross. Furthermore, we need to realize that only "through Jesus Christ" are even our very best deeds "acceptable to God" (1 Peter 2:5). In themselves they are never good enough to merit God's approval. As one old Puritan is reputed to have said, "Even our tears of repentance need to be washed in the blood of the Lamb."

The great theologian B. B. Warfield expressed it this way:

> *We must always be accepted for Christ's sake, or we cannot ever be accepted at all. This is not true of us only "when we believe." It is just as true after we have believed. It will continue to be true as long as we live. Our need of Christ does not cease with our believing; nor does the nature of our relation to Him or to God through Him ever alter, no matter what our attainments in Christian graces or our achievements in Christian behavior may be. It is always on His "blood and righteousness" alone that we can rest. There is never anything that we are or have or do that can take His place, or that can take a place along with Him. We are always unworthy, and all that we have or do of good is always of pure grace.*[19]

Note Warfield's emphasis on our continuing need to be accepted "for Christ's sake"; that it is always on "His 'blood and righteousness' alone that we can rest." The good news, however, is that we *are* accepted for Christ's sake, and our works are accepted on the same basis.

This is what Paul was saying when he wrote, "The life I live in the body, I live by faith in the Son of God, who loved me and gave himself for me" (Galatians 2:20). Paul knew his best attainments were never good enough, either to merit salvation in eternity or blessings in this life. For both, he relied on Christ and Christ alone.

Paul was no sluggard. He neither preached nor practiced "easy believism," the erroneous contention that because we're saved by grace, Christian discipleship is merely optional.

Remember what Paul wrote in Philippians 3:12-14:

Not that I have already obtained all this, or have already been made perfect, but I press on to take hold of that for which Christ Jesus took hold of me. Brothers, I do not consider myself yet to have taken hold of it. But one thing I do: Forgetting what is behind and straining toward what is ahead, I press on toward the goal to win the prize for which God has called me heavenward in Christ Jesus.

Paul pressed on; he strained forward. The imagery in his words is that of a runner pushing and striving with everything in him to break the tape, to cross the finish line first. Yet for all this effort, Paul lived by faith in Christ and His righteousness for acceptance by a holy God.

If you and I are to fear God by keeping His commandments, we also must learn to live by faith in Jesus Christ. Otherwise our obedience will degenerate into a works-based righteousness, and our fear of God will become a slavish fear. Only as we realize that we're "sons of God through faith in Christ Jesus" (Galatians 3:26), and that God the Father accepts us through Christ, can we follow God in filial fear, the loving fear of a child toward his father.

Loving Father in heaven, hallowed be Your name. I worship You today as I enter Your holy presence by the body and blood of Your Holy Son, Jesus Christ. You have not treated me as my sins deserve or repaid me according to my iniquities. You are "rich in mercy," and in Christ, through His blood, You have lavished upon me the riches of Your amazing grace. Thank You, loving Father! Hebrews 10:19-20; Psalm 103:10; Ephesians 2:4

I acknowledge before You that I can follow You and live this Christian life only by faith in Your Son, "who loved me and gave himself for me." Galatians 2:20

How I thank You for this "indescribable gift"—Your one and only Son. Since You did not spare Your own Son, but gave Jesus up for us all, I know that You will certainly, "along with him, graciously give us all things." 2 Corinthians 9:15; John 3:16; Romans 8:32

Thank You for my eternal life in Christ. Thank You for giving me faith, repentance, and forgiveness. You are truly "the God who gives life to the dead." Romans 6:23; 1 John 5:11; Ephesians 2:8; Acts 5:31; Romans 4:17

And Thank You for generously pouring out Your Holy Spirit upon my life. You are the God who "gives the Spirit without limit." And You give me not only Your Spirit but also Your Spirit's perfect prayers for me, in accordance with Your will. Titus 3:6; John 3:34; Romans 8:27

And so, by Your grace and Your power, I will follow You, O God!

FURTHER DELIGHT—
GREAT THOUGHTS
ABOUT GOD

Paul said to Timothy, "Train yourself to be godly" (1 Timothy 4:7). This word *train* that Paul used referred to the training regimen of athletes as they prepared to participate in the games of that day. In that context, the word carried connotations of commitment, focus, practice, and perseverance. All these characteristics are essential to following God and developing a God-fearing view of life.

Along with prayer and Scripture reading, an additional discipline necessary to this spiritual growth is the habit of thinking great thoughts about Him. It isn't enough to stand in awe of God as we read about Him. The Bible's word pictures of His greatness (such as those found in Isaiah 40, for example) should become a part of our daily thinking.

God provides illustrations in everyday life to guide our thoughts in this direction. I think of the common ant, which ordinarily is at best a nuisance to us. When Russian engineers designed their lunar exploratory machine, they used articulated legs (legs with movable joints) instead of wheels to traverse the moon's uneven terrain. What they had done unwittingly was mimic to a large degree the legs of a simple ant.

Even from His design of the body of a common insect we see the technological ingenuity in the mind of God from all eternity. All the most sophisticated scientific discoveries and inventions proliferating in our day are simply human beings thinking God's thoughts after Him. So instead of worshiping at the altar of science as our society does, we should turn our minds to God and see Him as the Master Scientist who first programmed all these things into His universe.

Develop the habit also of thinking great thoughts about God's providence. Become mentally aware of His unseen hand orchestrating all the events and circumstances around you. During my senior year in high school, I discovered inside our newspaper a single-column article no more than four inches long. It mentioned a navy scholarship program that provided a college education and an officer's commission upon graduation. I applied, passed the examination, and was accepted. The seemingly "chance" reading of that article buried in our newspaper was literally a life-changing event—and it was only the beginning. Several years later God orchestrated a "chance" encounter with another naval officer who would introduce me to the Navigators. In fact, it took two such "chance" meetings with him to get me to my first Navigator Bible study. Years later an offhand remark from a friend—"Jerry, you ought to try your hand at writing"—prompted me to get started on my first book. Were it not for that remark, which he doesn't remember making, you wouldn't be reading this book today.

My life is filled with such examples of God's unseen hand working out His plan for my life. I'm sure yours is also. Use these events as the mental fuel for thinking great thoughts about God.

Of course His unseen hand does not always work out events the way we would like. Disappointments happen every day. What do we do in such situations? We could stew and fret, as I confess I have done at times. Or we can bow in awe before God, whose infinite wisdom and sovereign power somehow, in ways we don't understand, cause all these events to work together for His glory and our good. This, too, is included in learning to meditate on God's providence.

Great thoughts about God will lead naturally to realistic thoughts about ourselves. We begin to realize how little we know, how uncertain and unpredictable life is, and consequently how little we're actually in control of anything. We begin to see that we're physically and spiritually frail and vulnerable, and that every second of our lives is lived at the good pleasure of God. As John Calvin wrote, "Man is never sufficiently touched and affected by the awareness of his lowly state until he has compared himself with God's majesty."[20]

Such an awareness of ourselves is spiritually healthy. Few things block our growth in fearing God as do feelings of self-righteousness and self-sufficiency. When we're pleased with our goodness and confident of our abilities, we tend not to stand in awe of God. But when we're shorn of our self-righteousness and stripped of sinful self-sufficiency, we're in position to fear Him.

Then not only do we fear God, but we bring Him pleasure: "His pleasure is not in the strength of the horse, nor his delight in the legs of a man; the LORD delights in those who fear him, who put their hope in his unfailing love" (Psalm 147:10-11). The strength of the horse and the legs of a man are pictures of the natural or human means we tend to rely on—they perhaps refer to military strength in both cavalry and infantry. But God does not take pleasure in those objects of our trust. Rather He delights in us when we fear Him and hope in His love and faithfulness. He wants us to stand in awe of Him and therefore to trust Him. We can do this only as we learn to think great thoughts about God. And when we do, we'll enjoy fearing Him.

"Great is the LORD." "O LORD my God, you are very great; you are clothed with splendor and majesty." Malachi 1:5; Psalm 104:1

In Your Scriptures we read Your question, "'To whom will you compare me? Or who is my equal?' says the Holy One."

The answer is that You, O Lord, are infinitely beyond compare! Isaiah 40:25

Praise be to You, great and mighty God. "Yours, O LORD, is the greatness and the power and the glory and the majesty and the splendor, for everything in heaven and earth is yours. Yours, O LORD, is the kingdom; you are exalted as head over all. Wealth and honor come from you; you are the ruler of all things. In your hands are strength and power to exalt and give strength to all." Now, my God, I give You thanks and praise Your glorious name. 1 Chronicles 29:10-13

I "acknowledge and take to heart this day that the LORD is God in heaven above and on the earth below. There is no other." Deuteronomy 4:39

Thank You, great and mighty God, that I can be assured of Your unfailing love throughout my life and for eternity. "I trust in your unfailing love; my heart rejoices in your salvation." Because of Your perfect love, O God, I will follow You. Psalm 13:5

I will follow You, O God. "Then will I ever sing praise to your name and fulfill my vows day after day." "I will praise you, O LORD, with all my heart." "Every day I will praise you and extol your name for ever and ever." "Praise the LORD, O my soul. I will praise the LORD all my life; I will sing praise to my God as long as I live." Psalms 61:8; 138:1; 145:2; 146:1-2

"O LORD my God, I will give you thanks forever."
Psalm 30:12

Praise and Thanksgiving

O MY GOD,

Thou fairest, greatest, first of all objects,
   my heart admires, adores, loves thee,
   for my little vessel is as full as it can be,
   and I would pour out all that fullness before thee in
      ceaseless flow.

When I think upon and converse with thee
   ten thousand delightful thoughts spring up,
   ten thousand sources of pleasure are unsealed,
   ten thousand refreshing joys spread over my heart,
   crowding into every moment of happiness.

I bless thee for the soul thou hast created,
         for adorning it, sanctifying it, though it is fixed in
            barren soil;
         for the body thou hast given me,
         for preserving its strength and vigour,
         for providing senses to enjoy delights,
         for the ease and freedom of my limbs,
         for hands, eyes, ears that do thy bidding;
         for thy royal bounty providing my daily support,
         for a full table and overflowing cup,
         for appetite, taste, sweetness,
         for social joys of relatives and friends,
         for ability to serve others,

for a heart that feels sorrows and necessities,
for a mind to care for my fellow-men,
for opportunities of spreading happiness around,
for loved ones in the joys of heaven,
for my own expectation of seeing thee clearly.
I love thee above the powers of language to express,
for what thou art to thy creatures.

Increase my love, O my God, through time and eternity.

—THE VALLEY OF VISION

NOTES

1. Charles Bridges, *An Exposition of Ecclesiastes* (1860, reprint, Edinburgh: Banner of Truth Trust, 1960), 309.

2. The context of Jeremiah 32:38-41 may cause some readers to think these promises are restricted to the restoration of the exiled Jews back to the land of Israel. However, the writer of Hebrews applies similar promises from Jeremiah 31:31-34 to the new covenant time in which we live. In addition the phrase "everlasting covenant" in Jeremiah 32:40 looks beyond the return of the exiles to God's eternal relationship with us.

3. John Bunyan, "A Treatise on the Fear of God," *The Works of John Bunyan,* 3 vols. (1875, reprint, Grand Rapids: Baker, 1977), 1:460. I have taken the liberty of modernizing Bunyan's writing for today's reader.

4. Bunyan, "Fear of God," 1:461.

5. Norval Geldenhuys, *The Gospel of Luke,* The New International Commentary on the New Testament (Grand Rapids: Eerdmans, 1977), 306-7.

6. Bunyan, "Fear of God," 1:460.

7. A. A. Hodge, *Outlines of Theology* (1879, reprint, Edinburgh: Banner of Truth Trust, 1972), 140-1.

8. J. I. Packer, *Knowing God* (Downers Grove, Ill.: InterVarsity, 1973), 76.

9. John Murray, *The Epistle to the Romans,* 2 vols., The New International Commentary on the New Testament (Grand Rapids: Eerdmans, 1994), 1:105.

10. John Calvin, *Institutes of the Christian Religion,* ed. John T. McNeill; trans. Ford Lewis Battles, 2 vols. (Philadelphia: Westminster, 1960), 1:41.

11. J. I. Packer, *Evangelism and the Sovereignty of God* (London: InterVarsity, 1961), 11.

12. John A. Broadus, *Commentary on Matthew* (1886, reprint, Grand Rapids: Kregel, 1990), 593, emphasis added.

13. Bunyan, "Fear of God," 1:458.

14. Other Scriptures addressing the issue of our relationships to those in authority are 1 Timothy 2:1-2, Titus 3:1-2, and 1 Peter 2:13-17.

15. F. F. Bruce, *The Epistle to the Colossians, to Philemon, and to the Ephesians,* The New International Commentary on the New Testament (Grand Rapids: Eerdmans, 1984), 382-3.

16. Meredith G. Kline, *Kingdom Prologue* (self-published, 1993), 41.

17. William Hendriksen, *New Testament Commentary* (Grand Rapids: Baker, 1962), 120.

18. Jan J. Müller, *The Epistles of Paul to the Philippians and Philemon,* The New International Commentary on the New Testament (Grand Rapids: Eerdmans, 1955), 91.

19. *The Works of Benjamin B. Warfield,* vol. 7, *Perfectionism,* pt. 1 (1931, reprint, Grand Rapids: Baker, 1991), 113.

20. Calvin, *Institutes of the Christian Religion,* 1:39.

SCRIPTURE INDEX